Understanding Prophetic EVENTS - *2000* - PLUS!

The Temple, Antichrist *and the*

New WORLD ORDER

END TIMES - *SERIES THREE*

DR. ALAN PATEMAN
Foreword by Dr. Ron Charles

BY DR. ALAN PATEMAN

BY DR. JENNIFER PATEMAN

AVAILABLE FROM APMI PUBLICATIONS, AMAZON.COM AND OTHER RETAIL OUTLETS

The Temple, Antichrist *and the*

New WORLD ORDER

DR. ALAN PATEMAN

BOOK TITLE:
The Temple, Antichrist and the New World Order,
Understanding Prophetic EVENTS-2000-PLUS!

WRITTEN BY Dr. ALAN PATEMAN
Paperback ISBN: 978-1-909132-73-3
Hardcover ISBN: 978-1-909132-99-3
eBook ISBN: 978-1-909132-74-0

Written in 1996, Released in (Copyright) 2018 Alan Pateman
Second Print/Update 2020

Published By:
APMI Publications
In Partnership with Truth for the Journey Books 27
Email: publications@alanpateman.com
www.AlanPatemanMinistries.com

Acknowledgements:
Author/Design/Senior Editor/Publisher: Apostle Dr. Alan Pateman
Editing/Proofreading/Research: Dr. Jennifer Pateman
Computer Administration/Office Manager: Dr. Dorothea Struhlik
Cover Image Credit: www.PosterMyWall.com

❖

Dedication

I lovingly dedicate this book to the Jewish people. In opening our eyes to the truth about the Jews and the Jewish people in regard to the Christian World, the Nations and the End Times, we will attempt through these pages to discover that truth and final out come for their destiny and ours. I pray that the Holy Spirit will give you insight into this very often misunderstood reality.

❖

Table of Contents

❖

Foreword

*Eschatology — the study of
the current knowledge of the End-Times**

In our modern society, the word invokes mental images of The Mark of the Beast, Tribulation, Armageddon and the last war to end all wars, and Final Judgment.

Although it has only been in the past 100 years that the word, *eschatology,* has been used as a noun to identify events that deal with the end-times or the time that immediately precedes the end of all things as we know it, teachings

*Note: This Foreword by Dr. Ron Charles is included in all four parts of this End Times Series (Series One: Israel, the Question of Ownership; Series Two: Earnestly Contending for the State of Israel; Series Three: The Temple, Antichrist and the New World Order; Series Four: The Antichrist, Rapture and the Battle of Armageddon).

associated with the event, theories proposed to predict the event and philosophies, *(both religious and non-religious)*, developed that attempts to explain or clarify the event dating back thousands of years.

The ancient Egyptians taught that the end of the world or the end of all ages, as they called it, would first be preceded by a great apostasy against their historical gods and then a massive return to the worship of the gods just before the end came.

The Assyrians believed that the end will be preceded by a great war on the plains of the Euphrates River between the armies of the West and the armies of the East and that at the height of the war, the sun god would appear bringing eternal peace and punishment to evil ones.

The Babylonians believed that the end will be preceded by a great leader who would cause all people to worship him, as the reincarnated Marduk. Then, when he had firmly established himself as Marduk, that Marduk himself will come and judge and destroy with intense fire, all those who were deceived by the great leader.

In fact, we now know that in virtually all developed societies for the past 5,000 years, from Egypt to Rome and from Assyria to Persia, there has been a belief by those societies that there will indeed be an end to all things and that this will be accompanied by wars and natural tragedies, judgement of all people, rewards for the believing benevolent and righteous, and punishments for the evil and or non-believers.

As it has been for thousands of years, so it is in our society today, with but one major exception—the Jews. It was in the early-19th century in England that a handful of theologians and bible teachers began to dissect the scriptures and discovered what they felt to be a uniform thread of God's compassion and benevolent consistency in dealing with the descendants of Abraham, that stretched throughout the bible from Genesis to Revelation; maintaining its constancy through wars, exile, natural disasters, genocide, and societal extermination.

This belief began to crystallize into a theological position that spread throughout Europe, into America and throughout the world, until by the mid-19th century it had become the accepted doctrine more than the exception in European and American evangelical and fundamental religious circles.

As this doctrine became more accepted in the late 19th century, eschatology specialists began to see how God's dealing with the children of Abraham over the past centuries and the horrors that they were forced to endure, has in fact set the stage for the modern development of the state of national Israel, which in turn is recognized as God's physical end-times epitome whereby these approaching events can more readily be recognized and chronicled.

Dr. Alan Pateman's four part End Times Series (*Series One: Israel, the Question of Ownership; Series Two: Earnestly Contending for the State of Israel; Series Three: The Temple, Antichrist and the New World Order; Series Four: The Antichrist, Rapture and the Battle of Armageddon*), not only seeks to bring the reader *"up to date"* with regard to present day societal eschatological convictions, showing how Israel is in fact, God's chosen instrument that will be used to chart and to instigate fulfilment of these long anticipated end-time events.

He also accurately traces the history of how the Jews through history have been used as God's instrument; how evil forces have for centuries, all the way up to this present time, sought to destroy these people, their mission, their purpose, and their unique position within the overall plan of God; and how the worldwide entrenchment of modern day apostasy, materialism and deception will immediately proceed the realization of these end-times events, anticipated for so many thousands of years.

Such a work has long been needed that successfully marries the past, especially that of the Jews and of the rise of anti-Semitism, with the events of the future, and clarifies the mysteries of eschatology so that those of us who await the glorious return of our Lord Jesus, can more easily understand and appreciate the inimitability of the exceptional days and times in which we live — the End Times.

Dr. Ron Charles
The Cubit Foundation
www.cubitfoundation.org

❖

Preface

In the year of 1996 my wife and I and our small son lived in the Tuscany area of Italy for the period of nine months. *(This is the duration of time before we moved to Italy in the year 1999).* And up to this time I had been preaching frequently throughout Europe, Africa and America etc., with a measure of success.

One would say that these early years of ministry were powerful and brought me in touch with many wonderful men and women throughout the nations. But one of the most difficult and evading revelations was the whole subject on

*Note: This Preface is included in all four parts of this End Times Series *(Series One: Israel, the Question of Ownership; Series Two: Earnestly Contending for the State of Israel; Series Three: The Temple, Antichrist and the New World Order; Series Four: The Antichrist, Rapture and the Battle of Armageddon).*

the End Times. I'd been to bible school and been successful in ministry yet I did not really have an understanding or should I say *any* understanding about the Jews, the Babylonian structure, the rapture etc.

Then one evening as it became seemingly my custom to read to my family and anyone else who *(team members etc.)* was there in the evenings. I would read from a particular book that God had inspired me to pick up or to take from my shelf. And it was then on one of those quiet, yet warm summer evenings in '96 that I began reading the biography written by Derek Prince, the husband of *(then his first wife)* Lydia Prince. The book was titled *"Appointment in Jerusalem."*

Oh, What a Wonderful Book that Is

I've cried as I've read the pages - as the Holy Spirit touched my own heart - my journey in ministry seemingly has similarities to this story - being led by the Holy Spirit along a life journey to fulfil the call of God. Her journey was to Jerusalem. My journey is to the nations. But wherever God is leading us, He always leads us by his Holy Spirit and we can learn through similarities, not only through the scriptures but also through the testimonies of others and of course the biographies that have been put into writing.

Let me make a statement here, the Holy Spirit is our teacher and He knows what we need to learn or teach us at any given time. Therefore I only read the books or listen to the tapes that He has led me to listen to or read that particular day. He knows what needs to be built into my soul and spirit man - He knows what I need to be fed upon to nourish my very being, He always knows what's up ahead as He's the one that's leading us.

But coming to a place of reading the whole of this special book, *"Appointment in Jerusalem"* God began to speak to me about the End Times. As I picked up a pen and began to make a few notes, I felt the Holy Spirit tell me to get up at 6 o'clock the next morning and begin a time of study because He wanted to reveal to me His plan for the End Times.

Six Weeks in God's Study

Every morning for the next six weeks I got up and the only place that was very quiet where I would not be disturbed was in a garage in the basement of our apartment block. Every morning I would be down there at 6 o'clock praying, studying and writing. Day after day, sometimes for hours at a time or until I felt a release and I knew that the day had finished and a new day would begin tomorrow.

Only there was a woman in the garage next door who had a big knitting machine, which she used to sit at most of the time. At first it used to disturb me with the noise of the thrashing back and forth of her machine! We never met, I never saw what she accomplished in her knitting over those weeks and she would not have had a clue that God Almighty was visiting one of His sons to reveal revelation on a very important subject that most Christians know nothing about.

Six weeks went past and what you have in this four part series on the End Times, *(Series One: Israel, the Question of Ownership; Series Two: Earnestly Contending for the State of Israel; Series Three: The Temple, Antichrist and the New World*

Order; Series Four: The Antichrist, Rapture and the Battle of Armageddon - also incorporated as five course syllabuses within the teaching curriculum of the LICU University) is a result of that time.

I can honestly say that this insight, understanding, revelation and impartation has changed my life. I have such a heart for the Jewish people, for Jerusalem as a Capital of Israel and for what God has in store for this time.

Of course you need to read and ask God to reveal to you by His Spirit, His truth. And together I pray with the same desire as Lydia Prince and ask you and every Christian to pray for Jerusalem.

Lydia wrote *"I suddenly came to see that we Christians have a debt that has gone unpaid for many centuries – to Israel and to Jerusalem. It is to them that we owe the bible, the prophets, the apostles, the Saviour Himself. For far too long we have forgotten this debt, but now the time has come for us to begin repaying it – and there are two ways that we can do this.*

First, we need to repent of our sins against Israel: at best, our lack of gratitude and concern, at worst, our open contempt and persecution.

Then, out of true love and concern, we must pray as the psalmist tells us, 'for the peace of Jerusalem,' remembering that peace can only come to Jerusalem as Israel turns back to God. God has shown me that from now on to pray in this way for Jerusalem will be the highest form of service that I can render Him."[1]

❖

CHAPTER 1

The Temple and the Antichrist

Time for a New Temple

The book of Ezra traces the story of the return of the people of God to the land of Israel after the 70-year captivity in Babylon *(approximately 537BC)*.

Ezra begins with the same words, which close the book of 2 Chronicles. They recount the decree of Cyprus, king of Persia to establish and restore the house of the Lord at Jerusalem. This gives us our clue to the meaning of Ezra, for it is a book, which recounts the method of God in restoring a heart, which has fallen into sin.

The book divides naturally into the ministries of two men: Zerubbabel was a descendant of David and therefore of the kingly line. Ezra descended from Aaron and is therefore a priest. This suggests immediately that in the work of restoration both a king and a priest are needed. The work of the king is to build, or in this case, to rebuild *(The Apostle's role is to build)*. The work of the priest is to cleanse *(The Prophet's role is to uproot, tear down, build and plant)*. **Not forgetting the Return of the People of God to their Home Land.**

Restoration of Our Soul

Digressing:

Restoration in an individual's life always requires these two ministries. There is the need to rebuild the character through recognition of the kingship and lordship of Jesus Christ in the human spirit. Such building involves the recognition of God's right to direct us and to change us according to His will. But restoration also involves cleaning. The soul is to be cleansed by our great High Priest, who is able to wash away our guilt, tidy up our past and restore us to a place of fellowship and blessedness before God.

End of.

Hands of God

Under Zerubbabel an early return of God's People takes place. This kingly descendant led about 50,000 people from Babylon back to Jerusalem. This is far fewer in number than those who have returned to the land of Israel in our own day, immigration in modern history is as follows:

1882 – 1903	*approx. 20,000 - 30,000*
1904 – 1914	*approx. 35,000 - 40,000*
1919 – 1948	*482,857*
1948 – 1951	*686,739*

1952 – 1954	*54,065*
1955 – 1957	*164,936*
1958 – 1960	*75,487*
1961 – 1964	*228,046*
1965 – 1968	*81,337*
1969 – 1971	*116,484*
1972 – 1974	*142,755*
1975 – 1979	*124,827*
1980 – 1984	*83,637*
1985 – 1988	*46,146*
1989	*24,050*
1/1 – 30/9 1990	*112,688*
1/1 – 30/11 1990	*approx. 150,000 from the USSR*

Making Aliyah from India

In the "Word from Jerusalem" magazine *(December 2013 edition)* it talks about Jews who are returning to Israel.

The International Christian Embassy Jerusalem is excited about welcoming to Israel another group of the Bnei Menashe community making *aliyah* from India in late December 2013. As with the group of 274 that arrived last January, the ICEJ again will be sponsoring the flights for the 200 Bnei Menashe expected to land at Ben-Gurion Airport sometime around Christmas Day.

Their journey home was made possible when the Israeli cabinet approved a resolution in October, which will allow another 900 members of the Bnei Menashe tribe to move to Israel over the next two years.

The government decision cleared the way for 200 Bnei Menashe to be brought by the end of this year, while 400 can come in 2014 and another 300 in 2015.

All of the immigrants will be housed in a private absorption centre run by Shavei Israel and will then be settled around the country.

The Bnei Menashe claim descent from the tribe of Manasseh, one of the ten northern tribes of Israel who were exiled by the Assyrian empire in 722BC.

Despite being cut off from the rest of the Jewish people for more than 2,700 years, the Bnei Menashe still retained their distinct heritage, observed Sabbath and kept kosher. Some 2,000 members of the community have already moved to Israel over the past decade. Another 7,000 are still in northern India awaiting their turn to come home. They live in the remote provinces of Mizoram and Manipur, and are already taking Hebrew classes and study courses to ease their adjustment to a new life in Israel.

The immigration process for the Bnei Menashe is not easy. It involves sorting through many details for hundreds of families, from arranging several days of flights to providing food and setting up housing, language classes and childcare programs in Israel.

Return of the Kaifeng Jews

According to some scholars, the Bnei Menashe community in northeast India is likely an offshoot of the Chinese Jewish community that began settling in Kaifeng, the capital of imperial China, some 2,000 years ago. These were Jewish or Israelite exiles from Persia who had worked their way eastward as merchants along the ancient Silk Road, all the way to its eastern terminal in Kaifeng. There are parchments and engraved pillars that document their presence in the area back to some 20 centuries ago.

At its height, in the Middle Ages, Kaifeng's Jewish community numbered as many 5,000 people, with rabbis, synagogues and various communal institutions. But the Kaifeng Jewish community eventually dwindled in numbers to less than 1,000 in recent generations.

There are still some 500 Chinese Jews left in the area, and many are now interested in making *aliyah* to rejoin the mainstream Jewish people back in the Land of Israel. The first Kaifeng Jewish family to make *aliyah* in recent times was actually sponsored on their journey home by the Christian Embassy around ten years ago.

More Kaifeng Jews are now taking Hebrew language courses and religious studies in preparation for moving to Israel, with assistance from Shavei Israel, our partner in the Bnei Menashe *aliyah*.

The ICEJ is helping to cover the flights for these Kaifeng Jewish families as well. For example, the ICEJ-Taiwan branch recently donated $25,000 for this unique *aliyah* operation.[1]

Increase in Jewish Immigration

The increase in Jewish immigration to Palestine during the 1900's was accompanied by an increase in Arab immigration. The original Arab population was not as large as Arabs contest today. Of a population of 4,477,000 *(Judea, Samaria and Gaza excluded)*, 3,659,000 are Jews, while 818,000 represent Muslims, Christians, Druze and others.

But the biblical record attaches great importance to this first return. Cyprus, the king of Persia, may have known of Isaiah's predictions concerning his instrumentality in the hands of God, for he gave <u>willing aid</u> to the Jews who returned, putting in their hands again the vessels of the Temple and giving them goods and animals *(Ezra 1:7)*.

In Double Dealing

Willing aid was not forthcoming when the British were involved. The appointment of a religious leader, the Great Mufti, Haj Amin el-Husseini, was appointed for the Muslims in Palestine.

He was a rabid Jew hater and stirred up aggression against them. During the war against Germany, he took a clear stand in favour of Nazism, and for several years, lived in Berlin. He was a friend of Hitler, Himmler and Eichmann, visiting concentration camps and counted on the help of the Germans to kill all the Jews in Palestine.

Germany, that agent aggressor, lost the war, but Britain never clearly sided with the Jews. It is said that during the war the concentration camps could easily have been bombed, but they never were.

Even the so-called *White Papers* that were drawn up to hinder the illegal immigration of Jews to Palestine could have been repealed, but they were not. Britain could have encouraged the formation of the State of Israel, but it never did. Perhaps Great Britain is not so great after all! It sided with the Arabs instead, and did everything it could to stop surviving Jews from reassembling in their homeland.

Britain's Fatal Mistake

At the end of the *Second World War* ships carrying survivors were forced to stop, so those on board were stopped from entering Palestine. Illegal immigrants were caught and penalised, and those who had just been freed from concentration camps in Germany, were concentrated in camps on Cyprus. Britain had made like many other countries a fatal mistake.

God says in Genesis 12:3, *"I will bless those who bless you, and whoever curses you I will curse; and all peoples on earth will be blessed through you."* Therefore through the actions of Britain it brought a curse upon itself; even though they had won the war and the *Great Victory* was theirs, still a curse fell upon Britain.

Within a few years, Britain lost its status as conqueror, its glory, its empire and its economy; appearing instead as a land full of difficulties and problems.

A Two State Divide

Britain had done its utmost to stop the Middle East Policy, which concerned the development of a Jewish State.

On November 29th, 1947, the newly formed United Nations voted in its general assembly that the Palestinian Mandate, which had been given up by Britain, was to be divided into two parts: A Jewish State and an Arab State.

The votes were 33 for, 13 against and 10 abstentions. The Jews rejoiced but the Arabs were furious; and Britain voted against!

Back in Ezra's time the desire was not just to return! When they came to Jerusalem it was the seventh month of the year and they arrived in time to celebrate the *Feast of Tabernacles.* This feast *(also called the Feast of Ingathering)* was the time when Israel dwelt in booths to remind them of their pilgrim character.

This feast also looks forward to the eventual re-gathering of Israel *(the time we are in now)* from their vast worldwide dispersion to celebrate the personal reign of the Messiah upon the earth in Great **POWER** and **GLORY**.

The careful list of those who have returned indicates that not only did various families and clans go back but also a company of priests. A smaller number of Levites, certain servants who were to assist the Levites in their service, and a number of people whose genealogy was somewhat uncertain.

Their first act upon returning was to build an altar on the original Temple site, in the midst of the ruins. Under the open sky they erected an altar to God and began to worship and offer sacrifice as the Law of Moses had bid them.

The second thing they did was to lay the foundation of the Temple *(Ezra 3:10)*. This work when finished was met with mixed feelings, for some of the people shouted with a great **shout** of joy. Others, including those who had seen the first Temple built by Solomon, wept with a loud voice so that it was impossible to distinguish the shouts of joy from the sounds of weeping *(Ezra 3:13)*.

Tears of joy mingled with tears of sorrow as the people saw the Temple being rebuilt.

❖

CHAPTER 2

Rebuilding in Jerusalem

When will the Temple be rebuilt in Jerusalem?

There is no revelation in the scripture as to whether the temple could be built before the rapture or tribulation, or in an interim between the rapture and the onset of the tribulation, says Dr. David Allen Lewis in his book, *"Prophecy 2000."*

"It could be during the first part of the Tribulation. All we know for sure is that it is in existence at the middle of the seven years, for that is when it is profaned by the Antichrist."

Interesting discoveries at the Temple site have been found. In 1968 Dr. Lewis was able to get back under the area where the *"digs"* were beginning. Now there is an arch cut into the wall that is perpendicular to the Wailing Wall.

One can go into, he says, a large vaulted room that has been emptied of debris of centuries.

"The Wailing Wall continues on north for some distance, under the built-up area. As you follow the wall you come to a grating in the floor. It covers a shaft dug down fifty-three feet to the original level of the time of Jesus and Herod. It is the opinion of some that the massive underground stones below the ground level could be remnant of the Temple of king Solomon. This must be taken as conjecture at this time.

Comforted in Jerusalem

At the south end of the wall around the Temple Mountain *(extension southward of the Wailing Wall)*, there is a large stone covered with glass for protection. This stone was uncovered within recent years. It has an inscription from Isaiah 66:14 chiselled upon it. Isaiah 66:14 is prefaced by the words *'Ye shall be comforted in Jerusalem...' (v13)*. Then the words of v14: *'And when you see this, your heart shall rejoice, and your bones shall flourish like an herb...' (KJV)*

Perhaps some pious Jew chiselled these words as the Temple was in flames, urged by the Spirit to do so. Then the stone was covered with rubble, only to be uncovered in recent times. Some of the Rabbis of Israel express the opinion that the stone is a sign that the coming Messiah is near at hand...

When **the Messiah comes he will superintend the building** of the final *(fourth)* **Millennial Temple** seen in a vision by the prophets *(see Ezekiel 40-48 and Zechariah 6:12)*."[1]

Rebuilding the Temple, according to Ezekiel 40-48, which significantly follows the story of the destruction of the Russian-led confederation as it attempts to invade Israel, the New Temple is necessary for the Antichrist's later appearance.

According to Revelation 11:1-2, a Jewish temple will be in existence in Jerusalem in the closing days of the age; it will be built by the time of the Great Tribulation.

> *And there was give me a reed like unto a rod: and the angel stood, saying, Rise, and measure the Temple of God, and the altar, and them that worship therein. But the court which is without the Temple leave out, and measure it not: for it is given unto the Gentiles: and the Holy City shall they tread under foot forty-and two months.*
>
> *(Revelation 11:1-2 KJV)*

Daniel speaks of the prince who would make covenant with the Jewish people and guarantee them religious freedom to make sacrifice and oblations *(Daniel 9:27).* That can only be done in the Temple, in Israel. The prophet also predicted that after three and a half years, the Temple would be desecrated by the prince, the Antichrist, who would invade the inner sanctum and proclaim himself God.

Too Hot Politically

In previous times people touring Israel asked their Holy Land guides and new Israeli friends, *"Will Israel rebuild the Temple?"* The answer was, *"No. Israel has no need for the Temple. The spirit of the nation is the only temple we need."* Even deeply religious people would dodge the issue. The issue was too hot politically.

Everyone assumes that the building of the Temple demands the destruction of the Muslim shrine, the Dome of the Rock, which allegedly stands on the very site of the ancient temple of the Jewish people.

I'm told that more and more Israelis are willing to speak of their aspirations to have the temple rebuilt. Not only the religious Jewish communities are showing an interest in the building of the temple but even the liberal Jerusalem Post, a secular newspaper, has carried several articles about the possibility of the rebuilding of the temple.

A quote from an article they published on February 11th, 1989, *"A Place for The Lord"* written by Pinchas H. Pell:

"The modern Jew found it difficult to face the binding obligation to rebuild the sanctuary, combined with the great dreams linked with it. He has suppressed the demands they make on him. He was hesitant to use religious language to describe the historic return to Zion and to national sovereignty.

There are indeed a few exceptions to this, as for example, 'the third Temple,' once used by Ben-Gurion *(in 1957)* or the excessive use of the prophetic terminology of the *'ingathering of the exiles'* during the years of mass aliya.

Maimonides Order of Events

Far beyond the formal commandment, the yearning to behold an actual concrete expression of a central religious and national vocal point permeates all Jewish history.

Another argument is that the rebuilding as postulated by Maimonides requires a certain order of events:

- Coming to the land
- Appointment of a king from the house of David
- Blotting out the descendants of Amalek; and only then
- The building of the Temple

The counter argument claims that while this is indeed the ideal order of events, the events themselves are not necessarily mutually interdependent and one must carry out whichever is possible at the time."[2]

Non-religious publications such as *"Time" Magazine* are beginning to pay attention to the Jewish aspirations for the building of the Temple. The 16th October 1989, edition carried an article titled, *"Time for a New Temple?"* The article is not entirely accurate in saying, *"Next week, Israel's Ministry of Religious Affairs will sponsor a first-ever conference of Temple research."*

Several conferences have already taken place in years gone by. There is a poster in Hebrew announcing such a conference a few years ago. It is possible, however, that Time was indicating that this would be the first conference officially recognised by Israel's Minister of Religious Affairs.

Here is the quotation from the Time article:

"Next week Israel's Ministry of Religious Affairs will sponsor a first ever Conference of Temple Research to discuss whether contemporary Jews are obligated to rebuild the Temple. However, several small organisations in Jerusalem believe the question is settled. They are zealously making preparations for the new Temple in spite of the doctrinal obstacles and the certainty of provoking Muslim fury.

Two Talmudic schools located near the Western *(Wailing)* Wall are teaching nearly two hundred students the elaborate details to Temple service. Other groups are researching the family lines of Jewish priests who alone may conduct sacrifices. Former Chief Rabbi Shlomo Goren, who heads another Temple Mount organisation, believes his research has fixed a location of the ancient Holy of Holies so that Jews can enter the Mount without sacrilege.

No group is more zealous than the Temple Institute, whose spiritual leader, fifty-year-old Rabbi Israel Ariel, was one of the first Israeli paratroopers to reach the Mount in 1967.

'Our task,' states the institute's American-born director, Zev Golan, 'is to advance the cause of the Temple and to prepare for its establishment, not just talk about it.' One difficulty is the requirement *(as in Numbers 19:1-10)* that priests purify their bodies with the cremated ashes of an unblemished red Heifer before they enter the Temple.

Following a go-ahead from the Chief Rabbinate, institute operatives spent two weeks in August scouting Europe for heifer embryos that will shortly be implanted into cows at an Israeli cattle ranch.

A New Temple is Essential

But historian *David Solomon* insists that a new temple is essential: 'It was the essence of our Jewish being, the unifying force of our people... but sooner or later, in a week or in a century, it will be done...'"[3]

(A red cow is on a secret farm location in Sweden. Attempts are being made to clone her in order to obtain a red heifer).

Grant R. Jeffrey has an understanding of **end-time and world events in light of prophecy** so we will let him take us on in this next part.

He says, "In November of 1990 government representatives, architects, engineers, rabbis, lawyers, and archaeologists met to discuss solutions to the practical problems connected with rebuilding the Temple. Researchers estimate the basic Temple structure could be built in one or two years. Naturally, the elaborate decoration work will take many years to complete.

The priests and the foundation stones will be cleansed with the waters of purification, just as they were when the exiles returned from Babylon. An altar for daily morning and evening sacrifices will be built in the area to the west of the planned Temple. Once the priests resume the daily sacrifice, the construction of the Temple itself will begin.

For the first time since AD70 serious people are considering the practical steps required to build the *Third Temple*. Naturally, a majority of Jewish layman and rabbis do not favour this project. However, a growing number believe they must rebuild the Temple to show the world that the Jews will remain in Jerusalem forever.

Even non-religious Jews are dropping their previous opposition to this project. While only a minority wants the temple rebuilt, the prophecies will be fulfilled at the appointed time when God puts this in the heart of the Chosen People. God's command has never been rescinded:

And let them make Me a sanctuary, that I may dwell among them.

(Exodus 25:8 KJV)

Locating the Building Site

Archaeologists are quietly exploring the elaborate honeycomb of subterranean tunnels, cisterns, and secret passages beneath the Temple Mount. Their discoveries have convinced many of us that the original Temple was located in an area some fifty yards to the north of the Dome of the rock. Documentary evidence from the Mishneh Torah's censored sections on the rebuilding of the temple tells us the Temple was directly opposite the Eastern Gate.

The dimensions of the Temple would place the Holy of Holies over the small structure called the Dome of the Tablets over fifty yards to the north of the Dome of the Rock. Evidence suggests that the original Ark of the Covenant rested on the *'Even Shetiyah,'* the foundation stone at the base of the Dome of Tablets.

This research, if correct, indicates the **Third Temple can be rebuilt without disturbing the Muslim Dome of the Rock.** Ezekiel prophesied that the Jews will worship God in their beloved Temple once again. The Lord promised;

I will set My sanctuary in their midst forevermore. My Tabernacle also shall be with them; indeed I will be their God, and they shall be My people.

(Ezekiel 37:27 NKJV)

The Third Temple

Jeffrey Grant goes on to say, "At the appointed time the Third Temple will be built in fulfilment of the bible's prophecies; possibly following the miraculous victory over the Russian-Arab army. After describing the War of Gog and Magog Ezekiel prophesied,

I will set My glory among the nations; all the nations shall see My judgement which I have executed, and My hand which I have laid on them.

(Ezekiel 39:21 NKJV)

The prophet's statement, ***"I will set My glory"*** may refer to the return of the missing Ark of the Covenant to the Temple. It will represent God's presence and unbreakable covenant. A curious prophecy of Jeremiah suggests that the Ark of the Covenant will return to the Temple before Christ sets up His Millennial Kingdom.

"Then it shall come to pass, when you are multiplied and increased in the land in those days," says the Lord, "that they will say no more, 'The ark of the covenant of the Lord.' It shall not come to mind, nor shall they remember it, nor shall they visit it, nor shall it be made anymore.

(Jeremiah 3:16 NKJV)

The prophet declared that, once the Messiah returns the Ark will no longer *'come to mind,'* nor will *'they visit it.'* Since Israel has not possessed the Ark for almost three thousand years, this prophecy suggests that the Jews will **'visit'** and **'talk'** about the Ark just before the return of Christ.

However, once the Messiah comes, the worship and attention will turn to Christ."[4]

❖

The Prince of Darkness will Defile the Temple

Abomination of Desolation

The Antichrist will violate his seven-year-treaty with Israel, stop daily sacrifices, and enter the Holy of Holies. *"Then he shall confirm a covenant with many for one week; but in the middle of the week he shall bring an end to sacrifice and offering"* (Daniel 9:27 NKJV).

The apostle Paul warned about the son of perdition,

> *Who opposes and exalts himself above all that is called God or that is worshipped, so that he sits, as God in the temple of God, showing himself that he is God.*
> *(2 Thessalonians 2:4 NKJV)*

Jeffrey says, "The fulfilment of Paul's prophecy may occur when he defiles the restored Ark of the Covenant by touching or sitting on the Mercy Seat."

This would surely qualify as the *"abomination of desolation"* spoken of by Christ in Matthew 24:15-35, "So when you see standing in the Holy Place *'the abomination that causes desolation,'* spoken of through the prophet Daniel — let the reader understand — then let those who are in Judea flee to the mountains.

Let no-one on the roof of his house go down to take anything out of the house. Let no-one in the field go back to get his cloak. How dreadful it will be in those days for pregnant women and nursing mothers! Pray that your flight will not take place in winter or on the Sabbath.

For then there will be great distress, unequalled from the beginning of the world until now — and never to be equalled again. If those days had not been cut short, no-one would survive, but for the sake of the elect those days will be shortened.

At that time if anyone says to you, *'Look, here is the Christ!'* or, *'There he is!'* do not believe it. For false Christs and false prophets will appear and perform great signs and miracles to deceive even the elect — if that were possible. See I have told you ahead of time.

So if anyone tells you, *'There he is, out in the desert,'* do not go out; or, *'Here he is, in the inner rooms,'* do not believe it. For as lightening that comes from the east is visible even in the west, so will be the coming of the Son of Man. Wherever there is a carcass, there the vultures will gather. Immediately after the distress of those days,

> 'the sun will be darkened,
> and the moon will not give its light;
> the stars will fall from the sky,
> and the heavenly bodies will be shaken.'

At that time the sign of the Son of Man will appear in the sky, and all the nations of the earth will mourn. They will see the Son of Man coming on the clouds of the sky, with power and great glory. And he will send his angels with a loud trumpet call, and they will gather his elect from the four winds, from one end of the heavens to the other.

Now learn this lesson from the fig-tree:

As soon as its twigs get tender and its leaves come out, you know that summer is near. Even so, when you see all these things, you know that it is near, right at the door. I tell you the truth, this generation will certainly not pass away until all these things have happened. Heaven and earth will pass away, but my words will never pass away."

Christ's words in Matthew 24:15 of *"Abomination and Desolation"* would allow Satan to present the Antichrist as *"god in the Temple."* An abomination is something religiously defiling. There is something so terrible about the Antichrist's action in the temple that the prophet Daniel could barely speak of it. The act of Satan's Prince of Darkness is so abominable that God will pour out His wrath from heaven when the Antichrist defiles the Holy of Holies.

Jesus warned His disciples, *"then let those who are in Judea flee to the mountains,"* (Matthew 24:16). Christ warned the Jews to literally flee to the hills when this abomination occurs. The wrath of God will be unleashed on earth at that very moment. This crisis will commence the Great Tribulation.

The Battle For The Temple

"When the Prince of Darkness defiles the temple many Jews will recognise that he is actually the false messiah. As the Jews rebel against his claims to be *'god,'* Satan will supernaturally empower his prince to fight against the *'holy people.'* He will use Satan's power in his attempt to destroy Israel as the Jewish remnant flees into the wilderness.

The Temple will probably be the initial battleground as the righteous priests battle to the death against the supporters of the Antichrist. Revelation 12:17 *(NKJV)* warns that *'the dragon was enraged with the woman, and he went to make war with the rest of her offspring, who keep the commandments of God and have the testimony of Jesus Christ.'*[1]

The Climax

And it will come about in that day that I will make Jerusalem a heavy stone for all the peoples; all who lift it will be severely injured. And all the nations of the earth will be gathered against it (Jerusalem).
(Zechariah 12:3 NASB)

In *"Appointment in Jerusalem,"* Derek Prince, gives his view on the subject, he says on the above scripture, that "At the time of writing this has not yet happened. But the possibility that it could happen is by no means remote. Indeed, with the international oil crisis, a conceivable rationale for such a universal gathering is provided - a crisis unimaginable in the days of Zechariah, or in fact until the advent of the internal-combustion engine in this century.

United Nations Resolution

In 1947, when the United Nations first voted to bring into being the State of Israel, they also adopted a resolution to put the city of Jerusalem under international control. This resolution has never been implemented: but neither has it been rescinded.

Suppose that the United Nations were to revive this resolution and then demand that Israel hand over to them, as the international authority, the control of Jerusalem. And suppose that Israel should refuse to do this. What then? If the United Nations should gather an international army to enforce its decision, against the resistance of Israel, the result would be just what Zechariah has predicted.

Of course, this is only one of various possible ways in which this final, universal attack against Jerusalem could come about. The permutations and combinations of international politics are so intricate that only the infinite wisdom of God Himself can foresee with absolute certainty the course that events will follow.

But at this point there lurks in the wings, waiting his cue to appear on stage, the sinister figure of a false messiah. Zechariah calls him *'the worthless shepherd' (Zechariah 11:17*

NASB). The New Testament writers call him *'the man of lawlessness... the son of destruction,' 'the Antichrist,' 'the beast.' (This last word means specifically a fierce, wild beast)*.

It is equally difficult to predict the precise role that this Antichrist will play in this phase of the drama. A man of unique intelligence and personal charisma, he will rise, through strange and dramatic events, to a position of dominance in world politics.

With his uncanny ability to manipulate men and nations, he will negotiate some kind to treaty with Israel, which will enable them to build a national temple in Jerusalem. This will gain him overwhelming favour in the eyes of millions of Jews. In fact, it will be sufficient to cause many of them to acknowledge him as their messiah — although this identification will have no basis in scripture.

Blasphemous Demand

Before the treaty with Israel has run its course, the treacherous deception of this Antichrist will be laid bare. Breaking his word to Israel, he will demand that he himself take his place in this temple and be worshipped there as God. Every sincere Jew will totally reject this blasphemous demand. In revenge, Antichrist will turn against the whole Jewish nation with a ferocity which will fully justify the title of *'wild beast,'* and he will use his worldwide influence to stir up war against the State of Israel and persecution against Jews in all nations.

Without attempting to unravel all the subtleties and deceptions of Antichrist's diplomacy, we move on to its final outcome, which as we have already seen, is clearly stated: *'all the nations of the earth will be gathered against Jerusalem.'* The defenders of Jerusalem will eventually be brought to the verge of total disaster: *'...the city will be captured, the houses plundered, the women ravished, and half of the city exiled...'* *(Zechariah 14:2 NASB)*

Indeed, grim disaster will confront Israel throughout the whole land. Two out of every three Jews in the land will be killed. But the remaining third, spared by divine mercy, will emerge to acknowledge the Lord as their Saviour and Deliverer *(Zechariah 13:8,9)*.

This will mark the climax of the period called by Jeremiah *'the time of Jacob's trouble.'* The Angel Gabriel tells Daniel concerning this period, *'...there shall be a time of trouble, such as never was since there was a nation (of Israel) even to that same time...'* However, both Jeremiah and Daniel promise Israel ultimate deliverance.

Jeremiah says, *'...but he (Jacob) shall be saved out of it.'* Gabriel tells Daniel, *'...and at that time thy people shall be delivered, every one that shall be found written in the book.'* Those that are *'written in the book'* are those foreknown and foreordained of God, corresponding to the one-third remnant of Zechariah.

Judgement and Mercy

'Then shall the Lord go forth, and fight against those nations, as when he fought in the day of battle' (Zechariah 14:3 NASB). At this point something will take place that is almost unthinkable to modern, sophisticated man. When all hope is gone for Israel's survival as a nation, God Himself will

intervene. The purpose of His intervention will be twofold: to bring judgement on the nations attacking Jerusalem and to show mercy upon Israel *(Zechariah 12:9,10; 14:3).*

This intervention of God against the army besieging Jerusalem will not be *'military'* in the normal sense. It will be a supernatural plague, affecting both the minds and the bodies of the attacking forces. Ultimately these will turn in total confusion against one another and will bring about their own destruction *(Zechariah 12:4; 14:12-15).*

At the same time the Lord will also move supernatural by His Holy Spirit upon the hearts of Israel, revealing Himself to them as the One whom they have rejected and crucified."[2]

> *And I will pour out on the house of David and on the inhabitants of Jerusalem, the Spirit of grace and of supplication, so that they will look on Me whom they have pierced; and they will mourn for Him, as one mourns for an only son, and they will weep bitterly over Him, like the bitter weeping over a first-born.*
>
> *(Zechariah 12:10 NASB)*

Dr. Jeffrey's Final Word

A final word from Grant R. Jeffrey, "Someone will kill the Antichrist with a sword after he stops the daily sacrifice. Some Jewish believer may break through his security and stab him in the head or neck. There are several verses that describe his assassination. Revelation 13:3 *(NKJV)* says: *'I saw one of his heads as if it had been mortally wounded, and his deadly wound was healed. And all the world marvelled and followed the beast.'*

After his satanic resurrection, the False Prophet will use this incredible event, possibly watched by billions on CNN, to convince the world that the Antichrist is the long awaited messiah.

Once the Antichrist consolidates his control of Jerusalem and the Middle East the False Prophet will force the people under the jurisdiction of his world government to worship the Antichrist.

From that point until Armageddon, 1260 days later, the world will be convulsed with spiritual and physical warfare between the forces of Antichrist and those Jews and Gentiles who will resist them."[3]

❖

CHAPTER 4

Revival of the Babylonian Religious System

Babylonian

The Mystery Religion of Babylon has been symbolically described in the last book of the bible as a woman "arrayed in purple and scarlet colour, and decked with gold and precious stones and pearls.

Having a golden cup in her hand full of abominations and filthiness of her fornication: and upon her forehead was a name written, MYSTERY, BABYLON THE GREAT, THE MOTHER OF HARLOTS AND ABOMINATIONS OF THE EARTH" *(Revelation 17:1-6 KJV).*

Babylon and the Bible:

Mentioned along with Babylonia more than 200 times in the bible, Babylon played a significant role in the life of the Hebrews. Abraham brought with him in his pilgrimage from this area, the language, culture and religion that left certain influences upon the stream of a Hebrew life.

Babylonia, along with Assyria, constantly affected the development of the Hebrew nation. Babylonia served as a second Egypt in influencing God's people. Through the enforced Babylonian Exile that followed the fall of Jerusalem and the collapse of Judean State.

Merodach-baladan:

Ruler of Babylon in the 8th century BC, carried on correspondence with Hezekiah, king of Judah *(2 Kings 20:12-19; Isaiah 39:1-8);* and Daniel and his three Hebrew companions were the captives of the Babylonians in the capital city *(Daniel 1:5).*

Isaiah 13:14; 21:1-10; and Jeremiah chapters 50-51 spoke of the coming fall of Babylon. They pictured it as an earth-shaking event in the magnitude of its impact upon civilised nations.

It Becomes a Desolated, Ruinous Heap

According to ancient Mesopotamian records, Sennacherib first invested the city and flooded it by means of canals to wreak vengeance on the city for its insurrection. Cyrus the great, Darius Hystaspes, Xerxes *(who punished rebellions in the city by destroying palaces, temples, and walls 480BC)* and finally Alexander the Great made conquest of the city.

Alexander planned to restore the city and make it the capital of his empire, but failed because of his untimely death.

Then in 312BC, Seleucus Nicator founded and fortified Seleucia on the Tigris, some distance from Babylon, and transferred the seat of the empire to that city. From that time, Babylon rapidly declined and never regained the status of a city.

At the beginning of the Christian era only a small group of astronomers and mathematicians were living in Babylon. Many of the cities in the vicinity, such as Hilla, used the sun-dried and kiln-baked bricks of the once great city to build new walls, houses and dams, as prophesied *(Isaiah 13:19-22; Jeremiah 50:23-26; Jeremiah 51:24-26).*

Rebuilding Babylon

Please note that to date, over $800 million has been spent in the rebuilding of Babylon by Iraq. Saddam Hussein has begun to rebuild the ancient city of Babylon. He and the Iraqi government have spent more than $800 million in re-building Nebuchadnezzar's Palace and Temples to the pagan sun god.

In Grant R. Jeffrey's book "**MESSIAH**" he has pointed out that *Saddam, though outwardly a Muslim, is actually a Satanist who has sold his soul to the devil.* Despite more than fifty known assassination attempts by individual Iraqis who hate him for killing their friends and families, Saddam enjoys satanic protection.

Although it is a violation of Islamic law, Saddam has allowed satanic rituals to be performed in Babylon. Every summer he holds a Babylonian Festival to honour the ancient pagan gods. **Babylon will become one of the Antichrist capital cities during the tribulation period. The other two will be Rome and Jerusalem.**[1]

The religious concepts and customs from previous generations that originated in Babylon continued on and were well represented in many nations of the world. Just what was the religion from ancient Babylon? And how does it all tie in with what John wrote in the book of Revelation?

Going back to scripture to the period shortly after the flood, we are told that men began to migrate from the east,

> And it came to pass, as they journeyed from the east, that they found a plain in the land of Shinar; and they dwelt there.
>
> (Genesis 11:2 KJV)

It was here that the City of Babylon was built and this land became known as Babylonia or later Mesopotamia.

Here the Euphrates and Tigris rivers had built up rich deposits of earth that could produce crops in abundance. But there were certain problems the people faced. For one thing, the land was overrun with wild animals which were a constant threat to the safety and peace of the inhabitants

(Exodus 23:29,30). Obviously anyone who could successfully provide protection from these wild beasts would receive great acclaim from the people.

Nimrod Appeared

Nimrod then appeared on the scene, a powerfully built man. He became a mighty hunter against the wild animals, famous in his time. The bible tells us: *"And Cush begat Nimrod: he began to be a mighty one in the earth. He was a mighty hunter before the Lord: wherefore it is said, Even Nimrod the mighty hunter before the Lord"* (Genesis 10:8-9 KJV).

Successful and famous, Nimrod the successful mighty hunter caused him to become a champion among those primitive people. He became *"a mighty one"* in the earth — **a famous leader in worldly affairs.** Gaining this prestige, he devised a better means of protection. Instead of constantly fighting the wild beasts, why not organise the people into cities and surround them with walls of protection? Then, why not organise these cities into a kingdom?

Evidently this was the thinking of Nimrod, for the bible tells us that he organised such a kingdom. *"And the beginning of his KINGDOM was Babel, and Erech, and Accad, and Calneh, in the land of Shinar"* (Genesis 10:10 KJV). The kingdom of Nimrod is the first mentioned in the bible.

The name Nimrod comes from *marad*, meaning, *"he rebelled."* The expression that he was a mighty one *"before the Lord"* can carry a hostile meaning *"against"* the Lord. The Jewish Encyclopedia says that Nimrod was *"he who made all the people rebellious against God."*[2]

The noted Historian *Josephus* wrote:

> *Now it was Nimrod who excited them to such an affront and contempt of God... He also gradually changed government into tyranny, seeing no other way of turning men from the fear of God... the multitudes were very ready to follow the determination of Nimrod... and they built a tower, neither sparing any pains, nor being in any degree negligent about the work: and, by reason of the multitude of hands employed in it, it grew very high... The place wherein they built the tower is now called Babylon.*[3]

Legend and Mythology

Basing his conclusions on information that has come down to us in history, legend, and mythology, *Alexander Hislop* has written in detail of how Babylonian religion developed around traditions concerning Nimrod, his wife Semiramis, and her child Tammuz.[4]

When Nimrod died, according to the old stories, his body was cut into pieces, burnt and sent to various areas. Similar practices are mentioned in the bible *(Judges 19:29; 1 Samuel 11:7)*.

Remember God has determined that His Church be *preserved* until the Second Coming of His Son, Jesus, at which time Satan and his followers will be destroyed. But Satan, knowing he has only a short time until his fiery judgement, seeks all the temporal pleasures that counterfeit godhead can bestow on him. So he is determined that the evil Mystery Religion he first set up in Babylon now grows and expands.

Christianity and Paganism

"Christianity came face to face with the Babylonian paganism in its various forms that had been established in the Roman Empire... Much persecution resulted. Many Christians were falsely accused, thrown to the lions, burned at the stake, and in other ways tortured and martyred."[5]

Over the centuries God has called His people out of the bondage of Babylon. Still today His voice is saying, "Come out of her, my people, that ye be not partakers of her sin!" *(Revelation 18:4 KJV)*

More than seventy years ago, Anglican Bishop Alexander Hislop observed that Satan has worked hard over the centuries on behalf of the Babylonian Mystery Religion that serves as his church:

Again and again has power been arrayed against it; but hitherto, every obstacle it has surmounted, every difficulty it has overcome.

Cyrus, Xerxes and many of the Medo-Persian kings banished its priests from Babylon, and laboured to root it out of their empire; but then it found a secure retreat in Pergamos and *"Satan's seat"* was erected there.

The glory of Pergamos and the cities of Asia Minor departed; but the worship of the Queen of Heaven *(Satan's false goddess)* did not wane. It took a higher flight and seated itself on the throne of Imperial Rome.

Babylon and the Catholic Doctrine

Hislop went on to explain how the Babylonian Mystery Religion continually rose above all attempts to put it down. **The early Roman Catholic Church, for example, incorporated many of its elements into Catholic doctrine and worship; Mystery Babylon lived on.**

Now following Nimrod's death, which was greatly mourned by all the people of Babylonia, his wife Semiramis claimed, *"he became a sun god."* Later, when she gave birth to a son, she claimed that her son, Tammuz by name, was their hero Nimrod reborn. **Claiming her son was supernaturally conceived and that he was the promised seed, the "Saviour."**

In the religion that developed, however, **not only was the child worshipped, but the mother was worshipped also!**

Much of the Babylonian worship was carried on through mysterious symbols - it was a *"mystery"* religion. Since the deified Nimrod was believed to be the sun god, fire was considered his earthly representation. Thus, as we shall see, candles and ritual fires were lighted in his honour. In other forms, he was symbolised by sun images, fish, trees, pillars and animals.

Paul the Apostle centuries later gave a description which perfectly fits the course that the people of Babylon followed:

When they knew God, they glorified him not as God... but became vain in their imaginations and their foolish heart was darkened. Professing themselves to be wise, they

became fools and changed the glory of the incorruptible God into an image made like to corruptible man and to birds, and to four-footed beasts, and creeping things... They changed the truth of God into a lie, and worshipped and served the creature more than the creator... For this cause God gave them up unto vile affections.
(Romans 1:21-26 KJV)

The reason for identifying the false church with Babylon is that the first organised religious rebellion against God began in ancient Babylon under the rule of Nimrod. Since Nimrod's rebellion, the Tower of Babel and centuries of spiritual rebellion, Babylon has been a key centre for satanic religion.

Roots of Babylon

It is said that virtually all of the perversions, heresies, false cults, and New Age religions could trace their roots back to the *"mystery religion"* of Babylon; when the city was destroyed after Alexander the Great conquered it *(around 300BC).*

Pagan priests and the mystery schools moved westward to establish their satanic rituals in Greece, Egypt and Rome. The religious title ***"Pontifex Maximus"*** was borrowed by the Roman Emperors from the pagan religious leaders of Babylon. These mystery schools developed similar satanic initiation rituals and meditation trances whose purpose was to allow a student to *"transcend"* his human limitations and *"become a god."*

This is New Age teaching at its best! Devoted followers continue to seek a satanic path to transcendence through mysticism and drug induced trances. Many would not use this language but still we hear of it every day, in such places as *"Rave"* parties, where to reach a more mystic plane, ecstasy pills are taken.

❖

CHAPTER 5

Mother Goddess

Semiramis, Nimrod's Queen

Wanda Marrs in her book, *"NEW AGE Lies To Women,"* says Semiramis, Nimrod's Queen, was clever and diabolical. "She spread far and wide the doctrine that Nimrod had not died. He had merely gone on to a heavenly abode where he sat as God of Gods and Master of All—a man-deity worthy of mankind's devotion and worship.

Semiramis' son, who later became her incestual husband was claimed to be the Son of God. This naturally made Semiramis herself the *'Mother of God.'* **This was the Satanic Trinity:** Father, Mother, Son—the prime gods and goddess of a perverse universe."[1]

Mary of Roman Catholicism (*a woman whom the Church has exalted above every other created being*), is said to be the Queen over all things, "That she might be the more fully conformed to her Son, the Lord of lords... 'Now, even as Christ sits at the right hand of God' (as seen in Hebrews 1:13). Mary sitteth at the right hand of her Son... Thus began... her heavenly glorification after the example of her only begotten Son, Jesus Christ... **Her dominion is the same as His; she is Queen of Heaven and of earth...**" Her glory can be compared to none but Christ's:

"...God has lavished upon this loving associate of our Redeemer, privileges which reach such an exalted plain that, except for her, nothing created by God other than the human nature of Jesus Christ ever reached this level."[2]

Roman Catholicism Teaches

From this exalted plane, Roman Catholicism teaches that Mary serves as "...Advocate, Helper, Benefactress and Mediatrix."[3] In this way she fulfils roles attributed in scripture to the Father *(James 1:17)*, the Son *(1 John 2:1; 1 Timothy 2:5)*, and the Holy Spirit *(John 14:16)*.

In accordance with the scriptures, the Roman Catholic Church teaches that when the angel Gabriel appeared to Mary in announcing God's plan for her to bear the *"Son of the Most High" (Luke 1:32)*, Mary responded, *"Behold the bond slave of the Lord; be it done to me according to your word" (Luke 1:38 NASB)*.

According to the bible, a miraculous conception followed in which Mary, though a virgin, *"was found to be with child by the Holy Spirit" (Matthew 1:18 NASB)*. At the completion, of this pregnancy, Mary gave birth to a Son and named Him Jesus.

Virginal Integrity Inviolate

The Roman Catholic Church teaches that the birth of Jesus was as miraculous as His conception, for, according to the Church, "Mary experienced no pain in giving birth to the child: *'To Eve it was said: In sorrow shalt thou bring forth children' (Genesis 3:6 KJV).* Mary was exempt from this law..."[4] The Church additionally claims, God preserved Mary's *"virginal integrity inviolate."*

That is, Christ was —

"...born of His mother without any diminution of her maternal virginity... just as the rays of sun penetrate without breaking or injuring in the least the solid substance of glass, so after a like but more exalted manner did Jesus Christ come forth from His mother's womb without injury to her maternal virginity."[5]

Furthermore, although she was wed to Joseph, the Church teaches that, following the birth of Jesus, Mary remained an *"immaculate and perpetual"*[6] virgin, abstaining from all sexual relations with her husband. The Church calls Mary *"the Blessed Mary, ever virgin,"*[7] the *"Virgin of Virgins,"*[8] and the *"all-holy ever virgin Mother of God."*[9]

The Mother of God

Though there is no biblical precedent for it, Roman Catholicism honours Mary as the Mother of God.[10] Since

Jesus is God, and Mary is the Mother of Jesus, then Mary must be the Mother of God, so the argument goes.[11]

The bible, on the other hand, never calls Mary the Mother of God for a very simple reason, God has no mother. As someone has rightly said, just as Christ's human nature had no father, so His divine nature had no mother. The bible, therefore, rightly calls Mary the *"mother of Jesus" (John 2:1; Acts 1:14)*, but never the Mother of God.

We begin to see perhaps where some of these doctrines came from, as Semiramis the so-called mother of god was also the head of a counterfeit religious system. Semiramis religious system was based on this unholy trinity which was laced with idolatry.

One of the most outstanding examples of how Babylonian paganism has continued to our day may be seen in the way Mary worship replaced the ancient worship of the mother goddess.

The story of the mother and child was widely known in ancient Babylon and developed into an established worship. **Numerous monuments of Babylon show the goddess mother Semiramis with her child Tammuz in her arms.**

Mother and Child Worship

When the people of Babylon were scattered to the various parts of the earth, they carried the worship of the divine mother and her child with them. This explains why many nations worshipped a mother and child — in one form or another — centuries before the true Saviour, Jesus Christ, was born into this world.

- The Chinese had a mother goddess called Shingmoo or the *"Holy Mother."* She is pictured with child in arms and rays of glory around her head

- The ancient Germans worshipped the virgin Hertha with child in arms

- The Scandinavians called their mother goddess Disa who was also pictured with a child

- The Etruscans called her Nutria, and among the Druids the Virgo-Patitura was worshipped as the *"Mother of God"*

- In India she was known as Indrani, *who was also represented with child in arms.* The mother goddess was known as Aphrodite or Ceres to the Greeks; Nana, to the Sumerians; and as Venus or Fortuna to her devotees in the olden days of Rome, and her child as Jupiter

- In Asia, the mother was known as Cybele and the child as Deoius

- "But regardless of her name or place," says one writer, "She was the wife of Baal, the virgin queen of heaven, who bore fruit although she never conceived"

- Devaki and Crishna; for ages, Isi, the "Great Goddess" and her child Iswara, have been worshipped in India where temples were erected for their worship

- In Egypt, the mother was known as Isis and her child as Horus

It is very common for the religious monuments of Egypt to show the **infant Horus seated on the lap of his mother.** In

Ephesus, **the great mother was known as Diana.** The temple dedicated to her in that city was one of the seven wonders of the ancient world! Not only at Ephesus, but throughout all Asia and the world was the goddess worshipped *(Acts 19:27).*

A further indication that Mary worship developed out of the old worship of the mother goddess, may be seen in the titles that are ascribed to her. Mary is often called *"The Madonna."* According to Hislop, this expression is the translation of one of the titles by which the Babylonian goddess was known. In deified form, Nimrod came to be known as Baal.

The title of his wife, the female divinity, would be the equivalent of Baalti. In English, this word means, *"My Lady;"* in Latin, *"Mea Domina,"* and in Italian, it is corrupted into the well-known *"Madonna!"*[12]

When the children of Israel fell into apostasy, they too were defiled with this mother goddess worship. As we read in Judges 2:13, *"They forsook the Lord, and served Baal and Ashtaroth" (KJV).* Ashtaroth or Ashtoreth was the name by which the goddess was known to the children of Israel.

It is pitiful to think that those who had known the true God would depart from him and worship the heathen mother. Yet this is exactly what they did repeatedly *(Judges 10:6; 1 Samuel 7:3-4; 1 Samuel 12:10; 1 Kings 11:5; 2 Kings 23:13).* One of the titles by which the goddess was known among them was *"the queen of heaven" (Jeremiah 44:17-19).* The prophet Jeremiah rebuked them for worshipping her, but they rebelled against his warning.

Saints or 'gods'

"Looking back again to the *'mother'* of false religion - Babylon - we find that the **people prayed to and honoured a plurality of gods.** In fact, the Babylonian system developed until it had some 5,000 gods and goddesses. In much the same way as Catholics believe concerning their *'saints,'* the Babylonians believed that their *'gods'* had at one time been living heroes on earth, but were now on a higher plane.

'Every month and every day of the month was under the protection of a particular divinity.' There was a god for each kind of problem, a god for each of the different occupations, a god for this and a god for that.

Even the Buddhists in China had their *'worship of various deities, as the goddess of sailors, the god of war, the gods of special neighbourhoods or occupations.'* The Syrians believed the powers of certain gods were limited to certain areas. As an incident in the bible records:

Their gods are gods of the hills; therefore they were stronger than we; but let us fight against them in the plain, and surely we shall be stronger than they.
(1 Kings 20:23 KJV)

When Rome conquered the world, these same ideas were very much in evidence, as the following will show:

- Brighit, was goddess of smiths and poetry
- Juno Regina, was the goddess of womanhood and marriage

- Minerva, was the goddess of wisdom, handicrafts and musicians

- Venus was the goddess of sexual love and birth

- Vesta, was the goddess of bakers and sacred fires

- Ops, was the goddess of wealth

- Ceres, was the goddess of corn, wheat and growing vegetation *(our word 'cereal' fittingly comes from her name)*

- Hercules, was the god of joy and wine

- Mercury, was the god of orators and in the old fables, quite an orator himself

This explains why the people of Lystra thought of Paul as the god Mercury *(Acts 14:11-12)*. The gods Castor and Pollux were the protectors of Rome and of travellers at sea *(Acts 28:11)*. Cronus was the guardian of oaths. Janus was the god of doors and gates. *'There were gods who presided over every moment of a man's life, gods of house and garden, of food and drink, of health and sickness.'*

Pagan Rome

With the idea of gods and goddesses associated with various events in life now established in pagan Rome, it was but another step for **these same concepts to finally be merged into the Church of Rome.**

Since converts from paganism were reluctant to part with their *'gods'* — unless they could find some satisfactory counterpart in Christianity — the gods and goddesses were renamed and called *'saints.'* The old idea of gods associated with certain occupations and days has continued in the Roman Catholic belief in saints and saint days, as the following table shows:

Actors	St. Genesius	August 25th
Architects	St. Thomas	December 21st
Astronomers	St. Cominic	August 4th
Athletes	St. Sebastian	January 20th
Bakers	St. Elizabeth	November 19th
Bankers	St. Matthew	September 21st
Beggars	St. Alexius	July 17th
Booksellers	St. John of God	March 8th
Bricklayers	St. Steven	December 26th
Builders	St. Vincent Ferrer	April 5th
Butchers	St. Hadrian	September 28th
Cab drivers	St. Fiarce	August 30th
Candle makers	St. Bernard	August 20th
Comedians	St. Vitus	June 15th
Cooks	St. Martha	July 29th
Dentists	St. Appollonia	February 9th
Doctors	St. Luke	October 18th
Editors	St. John Bosco	January 31st
Fishermen	St. Andrew	November 30th
Florists	St. Dorothy	February 6th
Hat makers	St. James	May 11th
Housekeepers	St. Anne	July 26th
Hunters	St. Hubert	November 3rd
Labourers	St. James	July 25th
Lawyers	St. Ives	May 19th
Librarians	St. Jerome	September 30th

Merchants	St. Francis of Assisi	October 4th
Miners	St. Barbara	December 4th
Musicians	St. Cecilia	November 22nd
Notaries	St. Mark	April 25th
Nurses	St. Catherine	April 30th
Painters	St. Luke	October 18th
Pharmacists	St. Gemma Galgani	April 11th
Plasterers	St. Bartholomew	August 24th
Printers	St. John of God	March 8th
Sailors	St. Brendan	May 16th
Scientists	St. Albert	November 15th
Singers	St. Gregory	March 12th
Steel workers	St. Eliguis	December 1st
Students	St. Thomas Aquinas	March 7th
Surgeons	St. Cosmas and Damian	September 27th
Tailors	St. Boniface	June 5th
Tax Collectors	St. Matthew	September 21st

The Roman Catholic Church also has saints for the following:

Barren woman *(St. Anthony)* beer drinkers *(St. Nicholas);* children *(St. Dominic);* lovers *(St. Raphael);* old maids *(St. Andrew);* poor *(St. Lawrence);* pregnant women *(St. Gerard);* Television *(St. Clare);* to obtain a wife *(St. Anne);* to find lost articles *(St. Anthony);* etc...

Everything considered, it seems evident that the Roman Catholic system of pagan saints developed out of the earlier beliefs in gods devoted to days, occupations, and the various needs of human life."[13]

Systems of Idolatry Flowed

Babylon had become the source from which all systems of idolatry flowed. Wherever the Mother Goddess flourished, idols were cast from bronze, gold or other metals and hewn from wood and stone. *Alexander Hislop,* in his remarkable 19th century work, *"The Two Babylons,"* documented how the Mystery Religion of Babylon assimilated all the other pagan religions throughout the nations. **It was also the principal spiritual enemy of the early Christian Church of the Book of Acts.**

This idolatrous religious system also showed up periodically among the Jews. God's wrath was repeatedly kindled at the apostate leaders of His chosen people who led their people into worship of Tammuz, Baal, Ashteroth, and Asherah, the Mother Goddess *(called the "Queen of Heaven" by heretical Jews).*

Isaiah said, *"How is the faithful city become a harlot!"* (Isaiah 1:21 KJV, and Jeremiah 10:1-14; 44:3; 44:15-25; Judges 10; Exodus 32:6; 2 Kings 23:11)

It was because of their abominations in despoiling the Temple by erecting images of the Queen of Heaven and by sacrificing their children to the fire gods of Babylon that God set about to punish the defiant Jews for their iniquity. First, in the 6th century BC, He brought them into captivity, in Babylon. Basically He turned them over to their sin! Then in AD70, Jerusalem was sacked and burned by the Roman General Titus.

The Jewish people were dispersed. Israel was extinguished as an independent Hebrew nation until almost 1900 years later when, in 1948, God miraculously restored the Jewish people to their ancient homelands in Palestine.

CHAPTER 6

Mother Goddess, the Sex Queen

The Queen of Heaven

The seduction of women is top priority on Satan's hidden New Age agenda, says Wanda Marrs. Her startling book is perhaps the first to completely reveal the New Age campaign to deceive and seduce women. Satan knows that if he can capture the mind and body of a woman, he then can quickly move to conquer her husband, her children, her entire family and circle of friends.

In her book **"NEW AGE Lies To Women,"** Wanda Marrs thoroughly documents the almost incredible Plan of the New Age leadership to foster sexual immorality by inciting lust feelings and creating seductive imagery in women's minds. She also explains how the New Age has successfully been able to damage and hurt women psychologically, break up marriages, lure our children into Satanism, cults and the occults, kill unborn babies, and undermine women's faith in God.

Wanda says in her book that the Mother Goddess *(Semiramis)*, "was also called the Queen of Heaven. She bedecked herself with jewels and gold and spread the doctrine that those who followed her and were initiated into the *'Mysteries'* would be prosperous, gain abundant material wealth, and enjoy sexual ecstasy as spiritual gifts from the gods.

Drunkenness and merriment was a prime feature of worship as revellers lifted their cups and chanted praises to the goddess. Sexual orgies then followed a revealing of the Mysteries, the secretive, satanic doctrines that were taught by Babylonian priests and priestesses. **Today, the sexual ritual and licentiousness of Babylon are back, introduced into modern-day society by the New Age."**[1]

It is interesting that in Italy, a country devoted to the Catholic Church, and committed to worship of Madonna is also a country steeped in sexual immorality.

Sexually Suggestive and Occult Scenes

Violence, illicit sex and the occult seem to go hand in hand in many rock songs. *"Heavy-metal groups"* take their listeners even farther out. One group, Judas Priest, on their album, *"Defenders of the faith,"* sing *"Eat Me Alive,"* the words depicting a girl being forced at gun point to commit oral sex.

Even more explicit are the words of songs by groups like W.A.S.P.

For example, the lyrics of one of their songs speaks of pictures of naked ladies lying on the bed and the smell of sweet convulsion and about howling in heat and finally, about committing the sex act, like a beast.[2]

Another clear example of the negative moulding power of pop idols are the recent claims made by a child-pornography expert. *In a report to the United Press International,* Judith Reisman said the following:

"Pictures encourage child pornography. You're dealing with an idol or heroine who carries with her a great deal of power and symbolism. For example, Madonna is seen as a desired being in society, so all young women want to be desired; they want to achieve.

If the nude pictures are described in popular magazines as appropriate, desirable behaviour, then youngsters, both girls and boys, will construe that to be the case. Large numbers of them will. Thus the pictures will encourage voluntary displays by youngsters. *That is not good.*

As far as the negative sexual problems, one news magazine reported that women all too often are portrayed as *'bimbos.'* They undress in silhouette; stretch out over car hoods and snarl like animals. Their dress includes fishnet and leathers."[3]

Madonna - A Pop Goddess

In 1989 Madonna's hit video *"Like a Prayer"* was replete with religious imagery and blasphemous overtones. The video begins in a church setting as **Madonna sensually caresses the feet of a statue of a black Catholic saint.** The icon sheds tears and comes to life. She picks up a dagger, touches the blade and the palms of her hands begin to bleed, emulating the superstition of *"stigmata,"* (a supernatural event which many erroneously believe signifies God's blessing upon an individual).

Madonna dances in a field of burning crosses in little more than a slip and is seductively kissed by the *"saint"* character. There is even a scene implying lesbian activity on the church's altar with a choir member!

Huge advertising mobiles hung in record stores across America, which peddled the *"Like A Prayer, LP"* with the inscription, *"Lead Us Not Into Temptation."* The singer went as far as to have patchouli, a West Indian fragrance, mixed with the packaging glue. This was for the *"Like A Prayer"* records and tapes, the marketing technique employed by Madonna.

Her publicist, Liz Rosenberg could hardly cover up the stench the video created.[4]

Modern-day Religious Depravity

Is this practice being restored today by the New Age? Below is the incredible, yet commonplace, true account of one women's modern-day return to the religious depravity of Mystery Babylon, *(taken from: Rickie Moore, "Goddess In My Shoes").*

"I knew spiritual did not exclude sexual. The tantric and Taoist approaches to spiritual sexuality appealed to me.

When I heard they emphasised the need for a man to keep the woman absolutely satisfied, I said sign me up! I wanted to become an enlisted.

We started off slowly, going to every available workshop, buying all the books written about it, and setting aside time...

Our first tantra course paid off. Now... I can have a *'jade garden'* or a *'lovely lotus,'* if I choose. His *(male body part - word deleted)* became a magic sceptre, a healing wand, or... jewel. Just singing, *'The jewel or the lotus'* was a turn on.

Through successive heights of ecstasy, we began to see visions with our minds, fill them with our hearts and dream them simultaneously. Yoga had prepared us individually for what we were experiencing together.

I was... perhaps the daughter of a thousand shining stars... the Shakti, the potent female energy that can change the face of earth... the portal to the past and the future, a sanctuary for incarnating souls, a pleasure field, a sanctuary for incarnating souls, a pleasure field of heaven, a sweet and beautiful flower, complete with perfume and nectar, surely worthy of being worshipped and kissed.

I thanked the stars then for all little girls, witches and crazy ladies... and for all little boys, wizards and holy men. I didn't need anyone to tell me I was a goddess... I knew it!

We began our ceremony at home... the altar was adorned with happy yellow face flowers, and bright burning candles that illuminated pictures of our loved ones. A single, long stemmed rose, my symbol for protection, reminded us that we could experience the mystical union with the universe...

We stood naked in front of the altar... then we took a comfortable tantra seat and gazed long and deep into each other's eyes...

Then, he was on his knees in front of me... I stood there looking holy and goddess-like in my new exotic belt."[5]

Sex Will Be Prominent In The End Times

The New Age Movement is *capturing tens of thousands* of women's souls through sexual lies. Sex, of course, is a big draw throughout society. Sexual images and erotic fantasies permeate our lives. We cannot turn on our television set or open the pages of a newspaper or a woman's magazine without coming face-to-face today with the graphic nature of sexual enticements and inducements. The New Age has mastered the art of inciting lust and unbridled passion in the breast of women.

Wanda Marrs says, "This is a religion that has as its core the same unholy practices that were prevalent in Babylon, Egypt, Rome, Greece and throughout the orient. In the centres before Christ, and in the first centres after Jesus' first coming, history is replete with the story and descriptions of the fertility rites and the sexual favours granted by the high priestesses in the temples of such cities as Corinth, Athens, Ephesus and Memphis...

Initiates celebrated the sex act with temple prostitutes, many of whom came from the aristocratic class - from the very cream of society.

The Cult of Diana

In Ephesus and elsewhere, the cult of Diana encouraged sexual license and sacred promiscuity. The idolatrous statue of Diana depicted her with a multitude of breasts, signifying her sensual nature. In Egypt, the sensual nature of the Mother Goddess, Isis, was also worshipped in fertility rites.

Hislop wrote that Semiramis, the Babylonian *'Queen of Heaven,'* led a licentious life and gave birth to many illegitimate children. Yet, the people grew to worship her as the *'Holy Virgin.'* In the Goddess religions, it was thought that sacred and ritual sex cleansed and purified; therefore the term **'Virgin'** was used, though its meaning is obviously far different than that envisioned by Christians.

The Roman emperors Nero and Caligula, who professed belief in Roman Gods derived from the Mystery cults of Babylon and Pergamos, were given to sexual orgies and incredible acts of debauchery and sexual depravity. *Homosexuality and pederasty (child sex abuse) was rampant throughout the Roman Empire and especially in Greece* where the normal practice of heterosexuality *(male-female relations)* was even sneered at by many of the affluent class and the nobility."[6]

Remember the New Agers who practice Tantric yoga actually believe that sexual union - in or out of marriage - brings spiritual communion with the divine energy forces of The Universe. Those involved in witchcraft and Satanism consecrate themselves to Satan through ritual sex orgies.

The Aquarian Conspiracy

Marilyn Fergusion, in the New Age classic *"The Aquarian Conspiracy,"* enthusiastically reports that for many New Agers, sex outside of marriage is the wave of the future. She says that the traditional view of fidelity and *"one man-one woman"* has given way to more *"liberated"* views. Quoting sociological experts, Ferguson adds that the New Age generation is free from guilt over sex![7]

Promotional Flyer, "1987 International Seth Seminar," referred to an international network of groups composed of the disciples of *"Seth,"* a demon, channelled by psychic Jane Roberts. This demon teaches that *"the universe is of good intent; evil and destruction does not exist... we create our own reality — literally — through the beliefs we hold, and therefore can change what we don't like."* In a recent leaflet published by the Seth Centre, the group stated its main ideas regarding sex as follows:

"We are in this to enjoy ourselves - spirit, mind and body. If it isn't fun, stop doing it!... It is natural to be bisexual. Heterosexuality, homosexuality, and lesbianism are equally worthwhile and valid sexual orientations... There is no authority superior to the guidance of a person's inner self."[8]

The Church of Witchcraft

Miriam Starhawk and her church of Wicca *(witchcraft)* no doubt agree with the followers of Seth. Starhawk's views of sexuality exactly parallel the wicked doctrines and fertility ritual of the Babylonian Mystery cults. Among these decadent views is the astonishingly depraved idea that sexual license is godly.

Starhawk expresses this view as follows:

"Sexuality is sacred because it is a sharing of energy, in passionate surrender to the power of the Goddess, immanent in our desires. In orgasm we share in the force that moves the stars."[9]

Starhawk teaches that witchcraft is the same as the Goddess religion. *"The Goddess,"* she says *"is the liberator... and her service is complete freedom."* She also emphasises, the connection for today's New Age woman with the sexuality of the Goddess:

"The naked body represents truth... the law of the Goddess is love: passionate sexual love... The love of the Goddess is unconditional... Any act based on love and pleasure is a ritual of the Goddess. Her worship can take any form and occur anywhere; it requires no liturgy, no cathedrals, no confessions."[10]

All this is a far cry from the truth, the bible makes it quite clear that those who indulge in:

Sexual immorality, impurity and debauchery; idolatry and witchcraft; hatred, discord, jealousy, fits of rage, selfish

ambition, dissensions, factions and envy; drunkenness,
orgies, and the like. I warn you, as I did before, that those
who live like this will not inherit the kingdom of God.

(Galatians 5:19-21)

The Goddess and Feminist Catholicism

Wanda Marrs says, "The extent to which the Goddess Religion of the New Age has penetrated many Christian churches and pseudo-Christian churches is remarkable, if not astonishing. Its invasion is especially notable...

To their credit, some Catholics themselves are very alarmed at the chain of events now occurring. In the conservative Catholic magazine *'Fidelity'* some time ago was a fascinating and revealing article, **'The Goddess Goes to Washington,'** in which Donna Steichen reported that in Washington, D.C, some 2500 people met for a *'Women in the Church'* conference.

Most were nuns, many of whom were clad in their habits and their veils. *The conference was an incredible event, a gala that affirmed the coming Goddess Religion!*

It appeared to be the consensus of the 2500 Catholic nuns, priests, educators and theologians present that Christianity needs to be *'corrected'* by incorporating the Mother Goddess and her rituals within its institutions. One Catholic sister, Madonna Kolbenschlag, gave a blistering address to the conference. She encouraged the participants *'in the name of our elder brother, Jesus'* to *'be a scandal'* to the current system of Christianity which promotes the male God.

Spirituality of a Different Kind

'*The myth of the Father God,*' said Sister Kolbenschlag, '*is largely a product of the Judeo Christian tradition. The holy one who is truth is beyond all images.*' According to Nun Kolbenschlag, whose address was widely and enthusiastically received by the audience, the male God of Christianity is a '*false God*' who has '*created the world we live in.*' It is therefore necessary, she urged, to create a '*spirituality of a different kind.*'

We must recreate a '*new myth*' of God, remarked Kolbenschlag. She then called for a return to the ancient Goddess religion. What she really desired was a combining of the Goddess and the God into one.

Women, Kolbenschlag stated, '*are clearly the catalyst for the formation of the new spirituality. It is women above all who are in the process of reversing Genesis, turning the myth on its head - and freeing their sexuality.*' Finally, to cheers and applause she trumpeted this conclusion: '*The holy one is breaking through the conscious of humanity as the Goddess.*'

The priests who assembled at this conference commended the female speakers. Bishop Francis Murphy, Auxiliary of Baltimore, stated, '*they are brilliant women.*' The Church, said Murphy, '*has to incorporate a lot of modern insights.*'

Such men as Bishop Francis Murphy and Father David Power and the other male leaders present were not at all embarrassed with the proceedings. They did not even blink when Sister Kolbenschlag remarked. '*Women have always experienced the inner connection of sexuality, affectivity, religious zeal, and the creative impulse. And so we have to ignore the Great Lie that denies this.'*[11]

Another Catholic theologian prominent in the Goddess movement is Matthew Fox. In his book, *"The Coming of the Comic Christ"* Fox writes that the Christian church is dying. It is dying, he says, because it has rejected *"the mother principle."* *"Though we love her (the Church) dearly,"* says Fox, *"we should let her die."*

Fox envisions a new church being born today out of the rubble of the Christian churches. A church that will gloriously uplift the Mother, the Goddess, the feminine principle. *"It is necessary"* he writes, *"that we all become our Mother's keeper. Mother Earth can be awakened,"* he assures us, though *"Her pain is great now."*[12]

❖

CHAPTER 7

Antichrist and the New World Order

The Spiritual Struggle for Planet Earth

Somewhere, perhaps in Europe there is a man, brilliant in mind, full of charisma working behind the scenes to gain political position. *Someone who will sell his soul* to get that position and Satan will be quick to give him the *"Kingdoms of this World."*

The bible points to this coming dictator as the *"antichrist"* destined to lead the world into terrible deception; **a period called the great tribulation.**

The lives of everyone will be profoundly affected, even destroyed, *culminating in the Battle of Armageddon.* Many say that now is the time, it is this generation, our generation, that has been called to live out our destiny during the period that the ancients called the *"birth pangs of the Messiah."*

With this in mind, I pray you will respond to this chapter, *"Antichrist and The New World Order"* not out of fear, but with an eagerness to understand this very important subject.

Prophecy foretells us two very important things about the final act where planet earth is concerned. **First** - The coming of the Messiah. **Second** - His ultimate victory over the Antichrist.

> *And I will put enmity between you and the woman, and between your seed and her Seed: He shall bruise your head, and you shall bruise His heel.*
> *(Genesis 3:15 NKJV)*

From Genesis to the last book of Revelation, there are continual predictions about the coming Messiah and the future Antichrist. In the beginning of the bible and the end, the focus is on the final destruction of Satan and of course his Antichrist.

The very first prediction about the Antichrist appears in Genesis 3:15, this is a remarkable promise. In this prophecy we can see the first mention of the virgin birth of our victorious Jesus, speaking of *"her seed."*

The word *seed* occurs normally in scripture in connection with the seed of the father, but this is the only place in scripture that the phrase *"her seed"* occurs. **This predicts that Jesus would be of the seed of a woman, and not the natural seed of a father.** This is important as we reflect on the above scripture, as the verse also reveals the future conflict between the coming Antichrist, the *seed* of Satan and Jesus Christ, *"her seed."*

Just as Jesus, the son of Mary, was unquestionably the *"seed"* of the woman, Antichrist in some mysterious way will most definitely be the *"seed"* of Satan. The prophecy foresaw the crucifixion of Jesus as Satan was allowed to *"bruise his heel."* But finally, Jesus ultimately defeats Satan, as it's said that **"her seed... shall bruise your head."** This also implies and predicts the long struggle between Satan and Israel.

Attempts to Rule as 'god'

In Ezekiel 28 we see the astonishing details of Satan from his creation:

He was originally in close proximity with God. He dwelt on the holy mountain of God; he was an anointed cherub. He was blameless in all his ways, splendid in wisdom, skilful in operation, perfect in beauty and the model of perfection; such was God's assessment of this once magnificent creature. This is so unlike the ugly depictions of Satan found in mediaeval art and the horror movies of Hollywood.

In Ezekiel's prophecy Satan appears under the prophetic title of the *"Prince of Tyre."* However the description clearly reveals that the subject is Satan, and not an earthly prince. "Son of man, say to the prince of Tyre, 'Thus says the Lord God: Because your heart is lifted up, and you say, 'I am a god, I sit in the seat of gods, in the midst of the seas,' yet you are a man, and not a god, though you set your heart as the heart of a god...

You were the seal of perfection, full of wisdom and prefect in beauty. You were in Eden, the garden of God... The workmanship of your timbrels and pipes was prepared for you on the day you were created... You were the anointed cherub who covers; I established you; you were on the holy mountain of God; you walked back and forth in the midst of fiery stones. You were perfect in your ways from the day you were created, till iniquity was found in you'" *(Ezekiel 28:2, 12-15 KJV).*

Satan then was not a grotesque monster with horns, he was not evil when created, *"he had the seal of perfection"* and was *"full of wisdom and prefect in beauty."* He was created as a *"son of the morning"* or *"morning star,"* Lucifer, meaning *"bright and shinning one,"* he was without sin. He appears to have been one of the greatest of the angelic beings, but not for long because he *"fell."*

> *How you have fallen from heaven, O morning star, son of the dawn! You have been cast down to the earth, you who laid low the nations!*
>
> *(Isaiah 14:12)*

Pride in the Heart

Pride was his downfall, pride of beauty and pride of position. We know God opposes the proud *(James 4:6)*. Pride is the very thing God hates, for in Proverbs 8:13 it says, *"I hate pride and arrogance."* However, Satan rebelled against God's will and decided to do his own. It is because of his pride in his beauty and wisdom, Satan rose in rebellion against God.

Isaiah the prophet tells us about the fall of Satan. "How you are fallen from heaven, O Lucifer, son of the morning!

How you are cut down to the ground, you who weakened the nations! For you have said in your heart:

I will ascend to heaven.
I will raise my throne above the stars of God.
I will sit on the mount of assembly.
I will ascend to the heights of the clouds.
I will make myself like the Most High."

(Isaiah 14:12-14)

Because of this, God threw him out of heaven, *"I was watching Satan fall from heaven like lightning" (Luke 10:18 NASB)*. Revelation 12:9 says, *"And the great dragon was hurled down — that ancient serpent called the devil, or Satan, who leads the whole world astray. He was hurled to the earth, and his angels with him."*

One thing is certain that he was present with the other *"sons of God"* at the moment of this world's creation. God asked Job, *"Where were you when I laid the foundations of the earth... When the morning stars sang together, and all the sons of God shouted for joy?" (Job 38:4,7 NKJV)*

Prince of the Power of the Air

The bible tells us that Satan is *"prince of the power of the air" (Ephesians 2:2 NKJV)*, because he had great power over the earth since the fall of Adam and Eve. Jesus refers to Satan as a king of an evil kingdom in Matthew 12:24-30.

Daniel 10:13 *(NKJV)* refers to demonic fallen angels that are associated with particular kingdoms on this planet.

But the prince of the kingdom of Persia withstood me twenty-one days: and behold, Michael, one of the chief princes, came to help me, for I had been left alone there with the kings of Persia.

This verse suggests the extent of the continuing spiritual warfare in the heavens that will ultimately culminate in the Battle of Armageddon.

Ephesians 6:12 *(NKJV)* warns Christians:

For we do not wrestle against flesh and blood, but against principalities, against powers, against the rulers of the darkness of this age, against spiritual hosts of wickedness in heavenly places.

Since the time of his sharp exit, *(or the Fall),* parts of the heavenlies and of course the earth, Satan has had access but does not have access or rule in hell. This is what some mediaeval mythology writers have suggested! The devil will not descend to hell until Jesus has cast him into the *"Lake of Fire"* after his final rebellion at the end of the Millennium.

John prophesied that when;

War broke out in heaven: Michael and his angels fought with the dragon; and the dragon and his angels fought, but they did not prevail, nor was a place found for them in heaven any longer.

(Revelation 12:7-8 NKJV)

- Some believe that when Satan is eventually thrown out of heaven to the earth he will totally posses the soul of the wicked, power greedy *"dictator who will take over the revived Roman Empire"*

- At that point *(not before)* this man, UN Official? Prime Minister? Politician? President? Ambassador? Religious Leader?... will become the Antichrist, Satan incarnate, from that moment he will force men to worship him as god

- You may ask the question so many have asked, will this Antichrist rule over the whole world? The answer is found in Revelation 13 and other passages

John writes: *"...all the world wondered after the beast"* *(Revelation 13:3 KJV).*

Power was given him over all kindreds, and tongues, and nations. And all that dwell upon the earth shall worship him, whose names are not written in the book of life of the Lamb slain from the foundation of the world.
(Revelation 13:7-8 KJV)

And he [Antichrist, beast] causeth all, both small and great, rich and poor, free and bond, to receive a mark in their right hand, or in their foreheads: and that no man might buy or sell, save he that had the mark, or the name of the beast, or the number of his name.
(Revelation 13:16-17 KJV)

Incidentally, who are the saints in verse seven against whom the Antichrist has power to make war? David Allen Lewis, in his book, *"Prophecy 2000"* says, "This would include the Jewish remnant, the 144,000 — and the multitude of Gentiles who are going to be converted as we read in Revelation 7:9 *(KJV), 'After this I beheld, and, lo, a great multitude, which no man could number, of all nations and kindreds, and people, and tongues, stood before the throne...'*

The saints of God simply means the people on earth at any given time who are living for God and have a salvation-redemption relationship with our Lord Jesus Christ."

All the Earth

Dr. Lewis goes on to say that, "The objection has been made that the terminology *'all the earth'* has been used in a limited capacity in at least one passage. In writing to the Corinthians, Paul does say that the gospel has been preached in all the world. Since we know historically that this refers to the Church's reaching the known world, or the Roman Empire of that period of time. With the gospel of Jesus Christ, therefore, any reference to *'all the world'* must refer to the Roman Empire only.

The conclusion is then drawn by a few expositors that the Antichrist will never rule anything more than the Revived Roman Empire. This is an absolutely unacceptable manner of interpreting the scripture. The context certainly puts a limitation on the use of *'all the world'* in Corinthians, as we know that Paul and the early Church didn't preach in North and South America as well as other yet undiscovered parts of the world. Nevertheless, *'all the world'* can be used in another context very literally.

Beyond this there is the fact that it says the Antichrist will rule over all the world. Revelation 13 also uses the terms *'all that dwell upon the earth,'* meaning this entire physical planet. Note the reference in Revelation 13 to all kindreds, and tongues, and nations.

Antichrist World Wide

I would further observe that if the terminology *'all the world'* is to be limited to the Roman Empire, then we have no business preaching the gospel in North and South America, Africa, or Australia, for Jesus said, *'Go ye into all the world and preach the gospel to every creature' (KJV).* Certainly He meant more than the Roman Empire. This is a proof that the terminology *'all the world'* can be used in an inclusive manner.

Finally, if *'all the world'* in Paul's day meant to him the known world of that time, then *'all the world'* and *'all the earth'* in Revelation must mean the known world of the future projected in this prophecy.

Yes, the Antichrist will reign world-wide. His power will not be as great in some areas as in others! There will be rebellions against him. He will not have the authoritarian power that some have pictured him as having on an entire worldwide basis, but he does have a worldwide coalition of nations, which he heads up. He leads all the nations of the world in the great conflict known as Armageddon.

At that time Jesus Christ will appear and defeat the powers of Antichrist. This prepares the way for the judgment of the living people compromising the nations of all the earth. This is to determine who will be allowed to enter the glorious millennial reign. And that Millennium is what we are looking forward to with high anticipation, not as a perfect age, but as an idyllic age.

The Millennium, after all, is God's inauguration to the eternity of eternities *'wherein dwelleth righteousness.'* There shall never again be any rebellion against God. Eternity, following the Millennium, is the time of perfection."[1]

❖

CHAPTER 8

Revived Roman Empire

Four World Empires

The Prophet Daniel foretold twenty-five centuries ago that four world empires would arise in turn to rule the world until the Messiah would appear to establish His Kingdom of righteousness.

The fourth beast shall be a fourth kingdom on earth, which shall be different from all other kingdoms, and shall devour the whole earth, trample it and break it in pieces. The ten horns are ten kings who shall arise from this kingdom.
(Daniel 7:23-24 NKJV)

Daniel saw thousands of years ago a revived Roman Empire rising in Europe. Following the fall of Rome a fierce sense of nationalism arose among the emerging nation-states in Europe. Many have tried during the last millennium to recreate the Roman Empire that once ruled from Britain to the deserts of Syria. European nation-states vigorously have resisted violent efforts of politicians, emperors etc., until now. Now in our lifetime, finally the Roman Empire is being revived.

European Economic Community

"In 1984 Jacques Delors, a brilliant French finance minister, was looking for a new challenge," says Grant Jeffrey. He goes on to say, "When he failed in his goal to become the Prime Minister of France, Delors was offered the presidency of the *lackluster European Economic Community (EEC)* as an alternative.

Despite the bleak prospects Delors believed the EEC had the potential to transform Europe and regain the ascendancy over the Americans and Japanese. He explained to the various member states that they faced a historic opportunity. *'Europe's choice is between survival and decline.'* The only solution was to break down the antiquated laws, customs, taxes and bureaucratic nightmares that held back business.

Delors had a vision of a Europe that would operate economically, defensively and politically as *one gigantic super state* while still allowing the cultural and language diversity necessary to satisfy the citizen's fundamental needs.

The president of the European Community Commission rules Europe from the thirteenth floor of the Berlaymont, the enormous headquarters office in Brussels, *(Belgium)* that serves as the political centre of the emerging ***European Super State.***

Jacques Delors plans for the European Community to become the greatest power on earth as we approach the new millennium. The goal is to regain the dominance Europe held for most of the last two-thousand-years from the rise of the Roman Empire till World War II.

Roman Law and Greek Spirit

In interviews he often speaks of the combination of Roman law and Greek spirit as the basis of the ***'European idea.'*** While his vision of European union is relentlessly futuristic, the plan will produce a modern revival of the ancient Roman Empire that spanned the continent as a powerful super state for almost a thousand years.

The 1992 plan for Europe represents an attempt to recreate the past at the same time it reaches out to an unknown future. Magazines in Europe often refer to the EC as ***'an embryo European government' and 'Jacques Delors' European Super State.'***

Grant Jeffrey says, "It is fascinating to examine the ancient prophecies of the bible concerning the rebuilding of the Roman Empire in the last days in light of the practical plans underway today to create this European super state.

Behold, a fourth beast, dreadful and terrible, exceedingly strong. It had huge iron teeth... and it had ten horns. I was considering the horns, and there was another horn, a

*little one, coming up among them, before whom three of
the first horns were plucked out by the roots.*

(Daniel 7:7-8 KJV)

Four Fundamental Proposals

In a pivotal meeting held in 1984, Jacques Delors made
four fundamental proposals that would transform the face of
Europe forever:

- The *first* reform revamped the EEC's institutions to
  provide a powerful political and organisational base
  for the community. He proposed major changes to
  empower the European Commission in Brussels with
  executive powers under his presidency

- The *second* reform created a common European
  Defence and Security Policy to eliminate military
  dependency on America

- Delors' *third* policy reform proposed a true European
  Monetary Union and a new European currency. This
  revolutionary idea was resisted by the nationalists,
  especially Britain, until 1989 when major steps were
  taken to facilitate the creation of a European financial
  currency called the European Currency Unit (ECU)

- The *fourth* reform was the most fundamental − the
  creation of an enormous *'home market'* included
  more than 320 million consumers. Delors created
  a truly *'unified single internal market'* that would
  operate as if the twelve nations were a single country.
  At the stroke of the pen a unified Europe became the
  world's largest market"[1]

Japan has taught America that the principle of unfettered competition in business can't hold its own against the joint ventures and close cooperation in which the Japanese engaged. Thus the Europeans have already begun encouraging their firms to join ranks as the only means of creating the home markets; rationalisation and research and development budgets needed to cope with the U.S and Japan.

Airbus Industries, the French, German, British and Spanish consortium, has already won itself a big chunk of the civilian aircraft market — once an American monopoly — and now the Europeans are scurrying to develop the next generation TV.

Thus 1992 aimed to create a new economic super power of 330 million people that can match the big two — the U.S and Japan — on even terms *(Jerusalem Post).*

The Following are Important Dates

- *April 18, 1951:*
  The Treaty of Paris establishes the European Coal and Steel Community

- *March 25, 1957:*
  The Signing of the Treaty of Rome establishes the European Economic Community, or EEC, also known as the Common Market. The original members were Belgium, Luxembourg, the Netherlands, France, Italy, and West Germany

- *1962:*
  The Common Agricultural Policy (CAP) is established

- *1968:*
  All internal tariffs are eliminated and a common external tariff imposed

- *January 1, 1973:*
  The Six become Nine as the UK, Denmark and Ireland join

- *1975:*
  Israel and EEC sign a Free Trade Agreement (FTA) under which both sides undertake to phase out tariffs on each other's exports of goods

- *1979:*
  The European Monetary System comes into effect, reducing exchange rate volatility between member currencies (Britain has consistently refused to join)

- *1981:*
  The Nine become Ten, with the entry of Greece to the EEC

- *April, 1989:*
  The Delors Report calls on the EEC to undertake a three-stage program aimed at achieving full economic and monetary union. The program was adopted in June, despite fierce opposition from British (at the time) Prime Minister Margaret Thatcher

- *1990s:*
  Austria, Cyprus, Turkey, Malta are all in the process of seeking membership. Speculation also extends to Hungary, Norway, Sweden, and Switzerland

- *December 31, 1992:*
  The target date for eliminating all trade barriers within the EEC[2]

This is not the final form of the Revived Roman Empire. One thing is for sure that the European leaders are not aware of the ancient biblical prophecies, which say that the reunion of Europe will most definitely prepare the way for the rise of ten nations.

This is concerning the re-building of the Roman Empire, also shown by God of the establishment of His Kingdom. This seemingly would happen in the lifetime of the very leaders who would re-establish the Roman Empire.

And in the days of these kings the God of heaven will set up a kingdom which shall never be destroyed; and the kingdom shall not be left to other people; it shall break in pieces and consume all these kingdoms, and it shall stand forever... God has made known to the king what will come to pass after this. The dream is certain, and its interpretation is sure.

(Daniel 2:44-45 KJV)

❖

CHAPTER 9

Everyone is Going New Age!

Millions Go Spiritually Blind

Fifty million people went to prayer simultaneously on 31st December 1986. How wonderful and what a powerful occurrence of modern times, God must be really moving! But it's sad to say, this was not brought about by the Holy Spirit, but the deceptions of the New Age Movement.

"The World Instant of Cooperation" was promoted by New Agers who believe that man is his own deity. It is said how could Christians be so gullible or spiritually blind, but millions get involved in this world-wide effort to begin the new phase of the establishment of the Age of Aquarius.

This prayer meeting started way back on the 31st December 1975 by anthropologist Margaret Mead and Robert

Mueller, former assistant secretary general of the United Nations. These prayer meetings became public in 1986 and continued annually, called the *Tri Millennial Countdown.* It was to continue until the year 2000 when apparently the New Age was to come down upon the earth.

Robert Mueller says:

- Religions should, accelerate their ecumenism and create common world religious institutions, which would bring the resources and inspirations of the religions to bear upon the solution of world problems

- Display the UN *(United Nations)* flag in all their houses of worship

- Pray and organise world prayers...[1]

There is no doubt that *one world religious and political leadership is the greedy, all-consuming goal of the New Age.* Not one day passes by that the New Age leaders somewhere in the world do not impress upon their followers the prediction that a new world order is coming - and soon.

Human World Order

Dozens of books have been written, hundreds of magazine articles published, and literally thousands of speeches presented detailing The Plan for this New World Order. One of the most revealing and thorough books is *"Toward a Human World Order,"* by Gerald and Patricia Mische. They were one of the five original co-sponsors of *Planetary Initiative for the World We Choose,* a group dedicated to world unity and a centralised government.

Their book is a detailed account of how a New World Order can be instituted, complete with an economic system embodying a *"whole earth personal identity system,"* as well as a plan for a New World religion. The most amazing thing about this book is that a Catholic-operated press published it.[2]

The Tara Centre, a *New Age group led by Benjamin Creme,* on April 25, 1982, ran a full page and in twenty major newspapers around the globe, including dailies in New York City, Washington, DC, London and Paris. The ad boldly proclaimed that the New Age Messiah, identified as the Lord Maitreya, was now alive and ready to assume his rightful place on the throne of world power. The ad bluntly admitted that this goal was at the very essence of The Plan:

"What is The Plan? It includes the installation of a New World government and world religion under Maitreya."

Five years later, 12th January, 1987, the Tara Centre published a similar full-page ad in USA Today, trumpeting the lie that *"The CHRIST is in the World."* The ad described the Lord Maitreya as *"A great World Teacher for people of every religion and no religion."* Britisher Benjamin Creme of the occultic Tara Centre in London is also a follower of the Tibetan, Djwhal Khul and Alice Bailey.

'Christ' Lord Maitreya!

According to Bailey, *"the Tibetan"* predicts a New World Order to be brought about when the *"Christ"* (not Jesus, but *Maitreya)* appears on the world scene. *This "Christ" or world leader is expected to establish a New World Religion to supplant the "false teachings" of traditional Christianity.*

World Goodwill offers for individual use *"The Great Invocation,"* a printed meditation which pleads for Maitreya to come swiftly so a new world can be built, man can recognise his divinity, and global peace and tranquillity can come to pass.

Evidently Maitreya is *(was)* to lead us into a new astrological era: The Age of Aquarius. Reverend Matthew Fox, a Catholic Dominican priest whose endorsement of paganism and nature worship has shocked many of the Catholic faithful, says we are *"on the verge of breaking into a new spiritual age."*

It is imperative, Fox warns, that we *"beware of the gods of the past"* — apparently a reference to the Holy Trinity: Father, Son and Holy Spirit. Fox says we must not look back at the fading age, but instead should embrace the New Age. *"To look back piningly,"* he cautions, *"is to commit idolatry."*[3]

In 1776 Adam Weishaupt, an apostate Roman Catholic, who had been raised by Jesuits, launched an organisation, the theories of which still linger and are manifested in a multitude of groups and philosophies today.

Order of the Illuminati

Mother Basilea Schlink, founder of the Evangelical Sisterhood of Mary, wrote, "On May 1st 1776, Adam Weishaupt, a professor of Canon Law, founded the *'Order of the Illuminati'* in Ingolstadt, Bavaria. Five years before that he was initiated into alchemy and witchcraft and under the cover of the Freemason Lodge in Munich he carried out occult practices.

He not only practiced occultism and Satanism, but also pursued political goals. The members of his order were, for instance, Voltaire, Mirabeau and Robespierre. In France the most fanatical group of Freemasons, the Jacobins, joined the Illuminati. They were the instigators of the gruesome French Revolution."[4]

The Illuminists stated several preliminary goals:

- The abolition of private property
- The abolition of the family structure
- The abolition of religion
- The abolition of national governments
- The abolition of inheritance rights
- The abolition of capitalism

The Illuminists saw these accomplishments as necessary for the establishing of their concept of a New World Order. *Of course the leadership of the Illuminati would become the rulers of the New Order.*

World Dictatorship

In 1927 *Vivian Herbert wrote,* "This was the secret entrusted to the adepts of the intermediary category, but hidden carefully from the initiates. The Areopagites or twelve disciples of Weishaupt alone knew what the aim of the society was — to establish their own world dictatorship after clearing out established institutions."[5]

New Age advocate Robert Mueller, former assistant secretary general of the United Nations, is highly respected within the U.S Catholic community as a Christian educator. Yet he has said, *"I am not so fanatical as not to respect faiths.*

I would never fight with another religion about the superiority of mine." Asked, *"What is the best religion?"* Mueller replies, *"You have about five thousand religions on the planet. You'd be dead before you studied them all to decide which is the best."*

Mueller is pushing for **"a convergence of the different religions"** on earth, believing that mankind should and will discover the *"cosmic and divine laws"* that unite all religions. He even claims that this is what Christ would want us to do:

"World-wide spiritual ecumenism, expressed in new forms of religious cooperation and institutions would probably be closest to the heart of the resurrection of Christ."[6]

Barbara Marx Hubbard, author of "Revelation: The Book of Co-Creation" joins Price in the god-man concept, John Randolph Price is the president, founder, executive director of *"Quartus Foundation for Spiritual Research."* Price and Hubbard believe that man is his own deity. Hubbard indicates that the chief sources of her inspiration were Teilhard De Chardin, Abraham Maslow, John Glen, Karl Marx, Sigmund Freud, and Albert Einstein. According to her, Jesus and Satan will one day return to God.[7]

Spirit Guides

Hubbard claims that her *"spirit guides"* gave her commentary on Revelation. Their message is explicit when they speak of the elimination of masses of people who fail to go along with their program. The spirit elders are ready to **"take action to cut out this corrupted and corrupting element in the body of humanity."**

Further, Hubbard seems to take comfort in the words of her spirit guide who says, *"Fortunately; you, dearly beloveds, are not responsible for this act. We are. We are in charge of God's selection process for planet Earth. He selects, we destroy. We are the riders of the pale horse, Death. We are coming to bring death to those who are unable to know God. We do this for the sake of the world..."*

Hubbard, an executive director of the World Future Society, a former Democratic Party nominee for the vice-presidency of the United States. She claims that what was done on December 31st 1986 **(Prayer meeting called the Tri Millennial count down)** could bring about a "Planetary Pentecost" that would be a *"Second Coming"* whereby men would transform themselves into *"Christ."*

John Randolph Price reveals that while *"peace"* will be the rallying cry for the New Age, it will not be the true motive behind the World Instant of Cooperation.

He wrote, "The Commission is not like the Peace Movement... December 31... will release so much love, light and spiritual energy into the race mind that the hypnotic spell for the majority of mankind will break up like a thawing of a frozen lake in springtime. And that will be the true beginning of the New Age... Yes, we have entered the New Age, but now we have the responsibility, the obligation, to create the civilisation of the Aquarian Age. That's our purpose."

The Unity of Church and State

The doctrine for the New Age World Religion, *"will be used as a test against governmental activities,"* which means that the state will enforce the doctrine that the New Divine Plan or set of doctrines will:

- "...be given out to mankind in the form of a Spiritual World Teaching or Religion. It will enable all men gradually to vision the nature of God's Plan for this earth and the part they will play therein. It will imbue them with a sense of purpose, of responsibility, and of spiritual security and maturity."

- The World Mind, the twelve-person council of world rulers, will impose on the world's population the *"new gospel"* that Paul warned the early Church about: a gospel of Satan. Acceptance will not be optional; the government will force people to obey. As The Plan so aptly and politely puts it, *"Progressive simplification and unification will... have taken place in the religious field."*

- *The New Age gospel will soften up the world for the appearance on earth of the fake "Christ" and* his disciples, the Masters of Wisdom. The World Government, also known as the World Mind, will give way to the Antichrist and his chosen hierarchy of demon-possessed men:

  "There will thus be the Spiritual Cabinet of twelve whose rightful head would be none other than Christ himself...

  He whom the Christians know as Christ, the Jews know as Messiah, and the Orient knows as Maitreya may eventually be recognised as one and the same Being. In this way could a *'World Religion'* develop quite naturally, and in harmony with a World Government."[8]

"Alders book even describes in great detail the work of the New Age *'Christ'* and his twelve-person *(mimicking Jesus' twelve disciples)* Spiritual Cabinet, who will see that **The Plan** is translated into reality on earth. They will not actually administer world government — subordinates will handle the mundane.

Instead, the *'Christ'* and the Masters of Wisdom will supervise new developments in science and psychology, insuring their *'spiritual purity.'* All of society will be homogenized into one Master Mind as provided for in the Divine Plan."[9]

"Religion would no longer be an *'aspect'* of human living but the almost unconscious foundation of every activity. Men would have become aware of the purpose and presence of God in every part of creation and themselves to such an extent that they would be incapable of separating *'religion'* from science, education, or government. The integration would have become complete."[10]

New Age Kingdom

Texe Marrs says, "The new society that results from this *'integration'* Alder ecstatically describes as heaven on earth. But any God-fearing Christian who has read the biblical prophecies can see that this New Age kingdom *is really a hell on earth.* This becomes most clear when we discover what is planned for currently existing religions in Satan's New Age Utopia.

Alder informs us that in carrying out the Plan the New Age *'Christ'* and his *'Spiritual Cabinet'* 'will represent a World Religion in which every denomination, creed and type of belief would find its place fully appreciated and without fear or favour.'

This pledge rings hollow when we find out what doctrines will be acceptable in this New Age system. Under The Plan, every belief is acceptable only as it agrees with the Mystery Teachings. Every iota of religious teaching must conform to the New Age bible that will be published by the New Age *'Christ.'*

The New Age *'Christ'* and his spiritual aides are to develop **'the new bible of a world religion, which will be the basis of future education.'** People will theoretically be free to practice the particular religion to which they previously gave allegiance. But in practice, the bible of the New Age world religion *'will become the framework for them all, assisting in their interpretation, stimulating them to move with the times and to cooperation amongst themselves.'*

The Antichrist will initially appear to respect many parts of the Christian and Jewish traditions as well as those of other religions. But eventually he will require all religions to conform to the New Age world religion.

Even decreeing that all churches, temples and synagogues are to become centres of **The One World Religion.**"[11]

❖

CHAPTER 10

Rome and the
Ecumenical Movement

The Extended Hand of Rome

Four hundred and seventy years after the Reformation many of the formerly Protestant churches are planning to reconcile with Rome and rejoin the church our ancestors *"protested"* against.

They *(our ancestors)* brought back the simple New Testament message of repentance and forgiveness; personal belief in Jesus and His once and for all sacrifice for sin on the cross, be all that is required for salvation.

They knew from scripture that all comes as a free gift from God, totally undeserved. *"And being made perfect, he became the author of eternal salvation unto all them that obey him"* *(Hebrews 5:9 KJV)*. They obeyed Him by believing the entire bible and *living and dying by it - and for it.*

In the book *"The Battle for World Evangelism,"* by Arthur Johnston, he says, "Emilio Núñez had the delicate and demanding task of spelling out the position Evangelicals should take toward the Roman Catholic Church in his paper entitled *'The Position of the Church Toward Aggiornamento.'"*

The Position of the Church

He claimed that this subject had been imposed on Evangelicals by the socio-religious realities resulting in the Post-Vatican II Conciliar Church. A marked difference exists between the Pre-Conciliar Church in liturgy and biblical renewal. Evangelicals could be most encouraged by the latter:

"Of all the changes in *Post-Conciliar Catholicism* there is none more promising of better things in the lives of thousands of Catholics than that related to the new attitude of the Roman Church toward the sacred scriptures. We must confide in the redeeming power of the scriptural revelation."

Faith comes by hearing, and hearing by the word of God.
(Romans 10:17 NKJV)

He believed that the renewal sought by John XXIII had become a revolution threatening the very foundations of traditional Catholicism.

Three well-defined tendencies have developed in contemporary Catholicism:

- *First,* traditionalism that closes the door to any fundamental change in doctrine
- *Second,* progressivism with its concern to reinterpret Catholic doctrine and effect a basic transformation in the structure of the church
- And *Third,* moderate Catholicism in the style of John XXIII, who wanted to renew the church within the context of traditional theology

This inner struggle for self-renewal is further complicated for Latin America Evangelicals by the unexpected hand of ecumenical friendship extended by the Catholics to the Protestants. Evangelical churches cannot, Núñez said, remain indifferent to this extended hand.

Inter-Evangelical Debate

Núñez then entered into the inter-evangelical debate that begins with the confusion created in the mind of one that is converted from Catholicism to Protestantism. It is natural to ask, *"If the Roman Catholic Church is our sister, why was I invited to leave it to embrace Protestantism?"*

Some Protestants favour closer relations with Rome; many others do not:

"Those who favour the ecumenical encounter say... that the Holy Spirit is moving in an unusual way in the Roman Church, and that the Evangelicals should be very careful in their anti-ecumenism, or they may be opposing the Work of God.

The other group asks if it is possible that the Spirit should approve an ecclesiastical relation that can compromise certain truths that He Himself has inspired. Besides, they say, if the Spirit has begun an extraordinary work among the Catholics, is it not certain that an anti-biblical ecumenism would hinder it rather than help it?"

Supporters of the ecumenical dialogue affirm that opposition to it demonstrates a serious lack of love toward Catholics. Opponents say that out of love for Catholics they desire to preserve the integrity of the gospel — and who has demonstrated more love *(for in the scripture love is not divorced from the truth)* than those who have given their lives as pioneers or martyrs in South America?

Catholic-Protestant Ecumenism

Another argument in favour of Catholic-Protestant ecumenism is the affirmation that the perfect church doesn't exit on the face of the earth. The reply to this argument is that although it is conceded that there is no perfect ecclesiastical community, this doesn't oblige anyone to unite with a church whose errors are evident in the light of the bible.

Evangelical uncertainties about the future of Catholicism should not pressure them into rejecting it, some say, for it is not known what is going on inside. Others disagree with the principle of *"waiting,"* because there are norms in God's Word ***"that guide the Church along paths of right doctrine*** *and morals, or must she depend only on the march of human events to determine her way?"*

The path of evangelical relativism, Núñez fears, and "the parenthesis of waiting may send many souls into an eternity without God, without Christ, and without hope..."

Aggiornamento should not lead to an unfounded optimism that minimises the post-conciliar differences and maximises the similarities, for aggioramento has not ushered in any fundamental changes in questions of tradition, authority of scriptures, papal infallibility, synergism, sacramentalism, mariology, purgatory, and prayers for the dead.

Our confessions are considered incomplete, and Roman Catholicism in *"the Church par excellence"* for *"the ecclesia semper reformanda"* is also the *"ecclesia semper eadem."* Núñez agreed with Francis Schaeffer's belief that Roman Catholicism was moving more and more toward a humanism that would make a relationship with ecumenical Protestantism more compatible.

The latter affirms that it is *"not necessary or even correct to evangelise Catholics"* because *"they are already incorporated into the redeemed community as a result of their baptism in the Catholic Church..."*!

The Evangelical must be positive in his teaching and practice but **"relevant proclamation of the Christian message includes also the clear and conclusive denunciation of error, wherever this threatens the life of the Church that Christ bought with His blood."**

Individual friendships with Roman Catholics are to be encouraged.

Ecumenical dialogue Discouraged

"In reality, to maintain burning in our hearts the flame of evangelistic zeal is one of the best antidotes against any theological or ecclesiastical movement that threatens the Church with paralysis in her missionary function."

The official translation of the final *"Evangelical Declaration of Bogota"* decided by a vote of the Congress that:

"In a continent where the majority are nominal Catholics, we cannot shut our eyes to the ferment of renewal within the Church of Rome. The *'aggiornamento'* faces us up both with risk and opportunity: changes in liturgy, ecclesiology, politics and strategy still have untouched the dogmas which separate evangelicals from Rome.

Nevertheless, our trust in the Word of God, the distribution and reading of which continue to accelerate within Catholicism, cause us to hope for fruit of renewal, and they present us with an opportunity for dialogue on a personal level. This needs to be an intelligent dialogue, and it demands from our churches a deeper and more consistent teaching of our own evangelical heritage, so as to avoid the risks of a false and misunderstood ecumenism."[1]

Rome and the Ecumenical Movement

Several years ago, Archbishop Runcie who was the head of the Church of England, told *"Time Magazine"* that he had

given a ring to Pope John Paul II as *"an engagement ring"* **in** view of the **coming marriage between the Roman Catholic Church and the Church of England.**

The Church of Rome has not renounced any of the fundamental doctrinal errors that provoked the Protestant Reformation in AD1520. The non-Catholic members of the union are making this Ecumenical union on the basis of theological compromise.

Even Catholic theologians admit that John Paul II is the most traditional Pope of this last century and the strongest advocate of worship of Mary, Queen of Heaven, Mother of God, as the *"co-redemptrix"* along with Jesus Christ.

A process of intense ecumenical dialogue has proceeded quietly during the last twelve years or so!

The church leaders are very close to healing the schism between the Greek and Russian Orthodox churches and the Church of Rome. Pope John Paul II has met with Buddhist, Muslim, and Jewish religious leaders from around the world. For the first time in history the Vatican has sought to establish ties with those other churches. The Pope has engaged in ecumenical religious rituals and services with other religions that would have been unimaginable for any previous Pope.

The danger today is that in opting for a man-made unity based on compromise and abandoning the Protestant Reformation and the truths of the scriptures that were sealed in the blood of martyrs, we are heading back to whence we came.

The Love Gospel

Michael de Semlyen says, today in Britain, there is a *"love gospel"* about, which confines itself exclusively to what is called *"the positive."* It is claimed that as long as Jesus Christ is proclaimed as Saviour and Lord, we are all as one in Him. Differences over doctrine must not be allowed to get in the way of this. They say, **"we can affirm truth, but not confront error!"**[2]

Even Evangelical Alliance, UK Director *(at the time)*, Clive Calver said: "More barriers need to come down if a true alliance of evangelicals in the UK is to emerge. There are thousands more with whom we wish to stand shoulder to shoulder."

Is this part of the New World Order? It must be said, those who point the finger and accuse anyone standing for *truth*, *(as being cultish or sect minded)*, are very often propagators of the so-called *unity at any cost,* which is part of the Babylonian church!

The Need for Prophetic Voices

A.W. Tozer said, *"Every century needs its prophetic voices. Those men who have been gifted by God with an incisive cutting edge to expose hypocrisy, denounce compromise, and call for holiness."*

He also said, "If THE CHURCH in the second half of this century is to recover from the injuries which she suffered in the first half, there must appear a new type of preacher. The proper ruler of the synagogue type will never do. Neither will the priestly type of man who carries out his duties, takes his pay and asks no questions, nor the smooth talking pastoral type who knows how to make the Christian religion acceptable to everyone.

All these have been tried and found wanting. Another kind of religious leader must arise among us. He must be of the old prophet type, a man who has seen visions of God and has heard a voice from the throne.

The Protestant Martyrs, godly and loving men, could have taken this same position of, peace at any cost, within the wider church of their day. They could have confined themselves to avoiding all controversy and to agreeing with their persecutors about many of the *'positives.'*

But, the scripture commanded them to *'exhort and convince by sound doctrine'* and to *'flee from idolatry.'* They obeyed; they saw the error and the idolatry, and as responsible leaders, as pastors trusted to guide their flocks into green pastures, they exposed and opposed it all roundly.

They could so easily have chosen to look the other way and concentrate on the many truths of the Christian faith, which was common ground. They could have elected to please men, rather than please God."

Papacy and the Antichrist

The Reformers saw the whole Catholic system as anti-Christian. Luther and Calvin went so far as to identify the Papacy with the Antichrist and they like Wycliffe, Tyndale, Matthew Henry, Spurgeon, Lloyd-Jones and many others saw the Roman Catholic Institution as Mystery Babylon, the Mother of Harlots, vividly described in Revelation 17.

The Spirit filled life is filled with testimony of experience which of course is not wrong in itself, but **"New Days, New Ways"** is a dangerous way of life!

"I well knew how many smooth arguments can be marshalled in support of the new cross," says A.W. Tozer.

- Does not the new cross win converts and make many followers and so carry the advantage of numerical success?

- Should we not adjust ourselves to the changing times? Have we not heard the slogan, *"New days, New ways"*?

- And who but someone very old and very conservative would insist upon death as the appointed way to life?

- And who today is interested in a gloomy mysticism that would sentence its flesh to a cross and recommend self-effacing humility as a virtue actually to be practised by modern Christians?

These are the arguments along with many more flippant still, which are brought forward to give an appearance of wisdom to the hollow and meaningless cross of popular Christianity.

The Golden Cross

He says *(Tozer)* "Doubtless there are many whose eyes are open to the tragedy of our times, but why are they so silent when their testimony is so sorely needed? In the name of Christ men have made void the cross of Christ. *'The noise of them that sing do I hear' (Exodus 32:18 KJV).*

Men have fashioned a golden cross with a graving tool, and before it they sit down to eat and drink and rise up to play. In their blindness they have substituted the work of their own hands for the working of God's power.

Perhaps our greatest present need may be the coming of a prophet to dash the stones at the foot of the mountain and call the Church out to repentance or to judgement...

Before all who wish to follow Christ the way lies clear. It is the way of death unto life. Always life stands just beyond death and beckons the man who is sick of himself to come and know the life more abundant. But to reach the new life he must pass through the valley of the shadow of death, and I know that at the sound of those words many will turn back and follow Christ no more.

But 'to whom shall we go?
Thou hast the words of eternal life' (John 6:68 KJV)."[3]

❖

CHAPTER 11

Experience or Truth?

The Charismatic Renewal

In his 1980 booklet, *"Charismatic Crisis,"* Anglican Renewal leader, Michael Harper noted that, "The Charismatic Renewal does not have a particularly good track record when it comes to concern for the truth. I am chiefly here referring to the truth about Christianity. Because of its emphasis on *'testimony'* at least in its formative years, it has tended to soft-pedal, even to ignore the truth, largely out of fear that it will divide Christians rather than unite them.

Many Christians have in the past been caught up in sectarian battles over words and doctrines, and it has been refreshing to defuse much of that.

Animosity sidetracks many of the big issues which previously divided Christians, and to find a new unity in one's experience of the Holy Spirit. But such a unity is bound to last only so long as one can survive on *'testimony theology,'* and that is not for long!"[1]

Experience the Extraordinary

Experience is spreading and has had a major impact in Britain. "In 1994, August, 1,500 people took part in the Ichthus *'Revival Camp'* at Ashburnham. Again extraordinary scenes were witnessed.

On the first night of the Grapevine bible week in Lincoln at the end of August, around 400 out of 3,000 began laughing during the talk. On the final evening, however, the preaching was totally disrupted as a number of those on the platform began convulsing with laughter. After a number of attempts to finish on a sober and serious subject the speaker was forced finally to cut his address short and return to his seat.

These effects on bible weeks were being monitored with interest and possibly alarm by some involved in planning the Spring Harvest weeks for April 1995, expected to draw 70,000 from across all evangelical traditions - both pro - and anti-charismatic.

The question was whether Spring Harvest's broad base of fellowship would survive if there were major disruptions. At a planning meeting of the worship leaders in September 1994 it was agreed that room would be made for what God was doing, while alternatives were provided on site for those wishing to worship in a more restrained atmosphere.

By the end of August 1994 all the bible weeks were now memories, but the effects on individual churches were continuing to accelerate. Ichthus made a decision to run extra 'receiving meetings' twice every week until the end of the year. Kensington Temple was committed to doing the same throughout September, while Pioneer People in Surrey pitched a huge tent in the grounds of a local school for two weeks, for meetings almost every day at which people like John Wimber spoke."[2]

Rolling in the Aisles

Martin Wroe of *"The Observer"* turned up at Queen's Road Baptist Church on Wednesday evening, 31st August, to see how things were developing.

He wrote; "The congregation was rolling in the aisles. Rolling and weeping and laughing and sometimes just lying there, moaning, wailing but in no pain. In other churches, they are occasionally barking, crowing like cockerels, mooing like cows, pawing the ground like bulls and, more commonly, roaring like lions. But mainly they are on the church floor, laughing.

Hundreds of congregations of normally staid churchgoers are left shaking uncontrollably, to all appearances revelling in some killer joke that only their fellow charismatics have been let in on.

To the consternation of traditionalists and sceptics, a primitive Pentecostalism is breaking out in sophisticated Anglican churches throughout the country.

Holy Trinity Brompton

Tens of thousands of British churchgoers are experiencing the *'Toronto Blessing.'* At Holy Trinity Brompton, more than 2,000 people - including recent celebrity converts, such as the former topless model and singer Samantha Fox - now attend services on a Sunday, including 1,200 for the evening service. The church is jammed to the rafters. Doors open at 5.45 for the 6.30 opening chorus, but there are queues of 500 outside by 5.30.

Converts are split on whether Britain is on the brink of an authentic religious revival - other revivals, such as that in Wales during 1904, began with ecstasy in the pews and ended with emptying of the pubs as the Holy Spirit fell on the unholy drinkers.

Mainstream Anglicans are horrified by the enthusiasm and unsophisticated antics of adherents, while others dismiss it as P.M.T - pre-millennial tension - or mass hysteria. But the official line of the Church of England is cautious approval.

Believers in Holy Ghost power, whether laughing like hyenas or roaring like lions, dismiss the ridicule, pointing to the 'drunken' antics of the first disciples in the Book of Acts, mocked for *'taking too much wine.'*[3]

Many people have been drawn to what is happening by intense feelings of spiritual emptiness, particularly those in leadership who have been giving out for many years.

A great desire for more of God, an overwhelming hunger, often comes before the experience - but when things happen, they can often surprise even those who feel they are prepared.

Personally I think there has been a need of a good laugh in the Church for years, but as a bible believer, *I would have cast some of those manifestations out in Jesus' name.*

"The Spirit-filled walk demands, for instance, that we live in the Word of God as a fish lives in the sea" *(A.W.Tozer).*

A Word of Caution

If one is not careful, as leaders we will allow the people to be opened up to channelling. We need the gift of distinguishing between spirits, operating within the leadership of our churches. The problem is that much of the phenomena is new to much of the Church.

In America people are paying $400 - $800 per person to see the same manifestations through their Spirit Guides.

Elliot Miller, describing and evaluating a growing social force, says, "As the channelling experience becomes increasingly common-place, it will generate more and more interest from such fields as sociology, psychology, and parapsychology. Already, scientific studies have been attempted, like the doctoral research of transformational psychologist Margo Chandley *[International College, Westwood, California]*."[4]

Chandley says, that often the questions such research attempts to answer would be of interest to all observers, regardless of their biases.

Chandley's study produced some interesting data:

"Childhood traumatic experiences were shared by twelve of the thirteen channels she researched. The experiences ranged from epileptic seizures, a shock from a fall, sexual or emotional abuse, neglect or abandonment by parents or peers. She said the channels withdrew into an interior life.

Also they all had had abnormal or mystical experiences - always when they were alone - between the ages of 3 and 11, Chandley said, *'Most had been raised Catholic. They were already open to the idea of hearing voices. Saints have lives in other dimensions.'"*

Elliot says, his own research has detected an additional pattern: in all or nearly all cases some form of trance-inducing or occult *(and thus biblically forbidden; see Deuteronomy 18:9-14, and so forth)* activity was engaged in prior to the alleged contacts from their spirit guides.

In most of the well-known cases, the prospective channel hears a voice asking him *(or her)* if he would be willing to serve as a channel for information needed to help mankind out of its present crisis.

Note: *Interestingly, the contacted is often first troubled by the thought, "this is the devil." But the enticer's charm and seeming benevolence eventually win him or her over.*

But with channelling rising in popularity, a new scenario is becoming common: the initial efforts to establish contact are made on the human side by New Agers who have taken courses and/or read books on how to become a channel.

One such book, *"Opening to Channel"* describes the feelings associated with the channelling experience:

"Some people go through shudders or strong physical sensations as guides come in, but that is rare. These sensations can usually be eliminated as the person opens and learns to handle the larger energy flowing through his or her body. The most common sensations are HEAT and TINGLING."[5]

Christian Democracy

David Alton, whose battle against abortion in Parliament *(which I commend)* has won him great influence among evangelicals, was baptised by Franciscan monks and educated by the Sisters of Mercy and the Jesuits. According to Sunday Times writer Elizabeth Grice, Alton mocks the suggestion that he is a member of the Roman Catholic Mafia, taking his orders from Rome.

He describes himself as an Ecumenical Christian and like Charles Whitehead is married to an Anglican; and although he worships mainly at Liverpool's Roman Catholic Cathedral, he also attends a Church of England church in Edge Hill.

Many of the people who attended the rally which launched the *"New Movement of Christian Democracy"* in London, in November 1990, were pro-lifers who had made contact with David Alton's office during the Abortion Amendment Campaign, according to the Catholic newspaper, *The Universe.* Founded by Mr Alton and his Roman Catholic fellow MP, Ken Hargreaves, the movement aims to *"bring Christian values back into British political life."*

As well as *"to forge a valuable link with other Christian parties on the European mainland, such as those in Italy, Germany, Belgium, Luxembourg, Holland and Austria, together with their new counterparts in Hungary, Poland and Czechoslovakia."*[6]

Michael de Semlyen says, "There is little doubt but that the solid post-war success of the Christian Democratic Parties in Europe has convinced the Vatican that Social Democracy with a Christian label is the way forward, especially after the spectacular failure of Communism.

Catholic Action

The Jesuits, using *'Catholic Action'* and other forms of political activity and pressure, have played the key role in bringing about these successes in Western Europe and are poised to do the same in the East.

The Pope has specifically called on the Society of Jesus *(Jesuits)* to train priests for Eastern Europe to give the ROMAN CATHOLIC CHURCH what *"The European"* described as 'a leading role in the political reform of Eastern Europe.'"[7]

Time Magazine reported, in the same month that "Jesuit experts met in Rome in mid-December 1990 to plan this job. The Jesuits, currently training 1.8 million students in colleges and schools throughout the world, are regarded as *'the intellectual elite who educate the cream of Catholic Society, as well as being the largest missionary body in the Catholic Church.'"*[8]

Whereas Christian Democracy has brought many dividends to the Vatican in Europe, the strategy for Central

America implemented by the Jesuits has been more reliant on Marxism and Liberation Theology.

The Denver, Colorado-based organisation "Concerned Christians" drew attention to Jesuit activities in Latin American countries in 1989; "Jesuits occupy high positions in the Sandinista government in Nicaragua, despite its Marxist leanings," reported the magazine US News and World Report.

Others, having set up a network of *worker priests,* are deeply involved in revolutionary movements in El Salvador, Guatemala, Brazil and elsewhere.

❖

CHAPTER 12

Danger of Wrong Alignment

Jesuits - Defenders of Catholicism

Stonyhurst College the Jesuit school of Charles Whitehead. In a testimony that he gives on the "Full Gospel Business Men's Fellowship International" circuit, has revealed and affirmed his Jesuit background. He is married to an Anglican and heads the *"Catholic Charismatic Renewal Organisation"* in Britain and also for Northern Europe, for which he regularly reports to the Vatican.

His parachurch activities, especially his role as President of an FGBMFI Chapter have greatly influenced many Protestant leaders, who have been led in an ecumenical direction by him.

Appearances on television in 1991 point the way to his arrival on the national stage as Catholic lay leader in the Charismatic church as it emerges as a serious force under George Carey's ecumenical leadership *(remember Jesuits are - defenders of Catholicism).*

Decade of Evangelisation

On 6th January 1991, Epiphany Sunday, The Decade of Evangelism was launched at more than 30,000 church services throughout the country. A Novena of Prayer to inaugurate the *"Decade"* had commenced with a pilgrimage to the Shrine of Our Lady of Walsingham on 29th December 1990.

Alongside the Decade of Evangelism as part of the interchurch process is the Roman Catholic Decade of Evangelisation or Evangelisation 2000, also formally brought into being on the day which celebrates Christ's manifestation to the Gentiles.

The original idea and initiative taken for the Decade of Evangelisation came from Franciscan Friar Tom Forrest, who now *(at the time of writing this book)* directs Evangelisation 2000 in the Vatican, with Irishman, Friar Jim Birmingham.

It was based on the Vision that more than one half of the World's population would be presented to Jesus, as Christians for His 2,000th birthday. This vision was shared and confirmed at Nairobi, Kenya, in 1983 between Larry Christenson, Michael Harper and Tom Forrest.

The Decade of Evangelism was given its European launch at Acts '86, when the Anglican Charismatic leader Michael Harper sent a message to Pope John Paul II, via Tom Forrest. "We're with you for a united Evangelisation of Europe" *(are we wishing to stand shoulder to shoulder with those Evangelicals who worship, "Queen of Heaven?")*

The campaign is highly structured with key Vatican departments involved and most countries have a National Service Committee reporting in to the Vatican. Tom Forrest heads the office in Rome alongside fellow American Ken Metz, head of the international Catholic Charismatic Renewal office.

But as Forrest said in 1989, pointing to the weighty backing of the project, *"Everything is now receiving guidance from Secretary of State, Cardinal Agostino Casaroli, and from the Vatican Secretariat of Christian Unity."*

United with Roman Catholics?

Gatherings like Acts '86, in 1987 Congress in New Orleans, 1988 in Chicago, Berlin, and Washington for Jesus 1990 in Indianapolis and in Berne, through other Charismatic leaders like John Wimber, Bob Mumford, Larry Christenson, Vinson Synan and Michael Harper have given the Vatican the same message, that they are united with Roman Catholics in the plan to evangelise the world. They have also given considerable impetus to the launch of *"Evangelisation 2000"* among Pentecostals and Charismatics.

Can so many Leaders be taken in by Catholic deception? John Wimber, an enthusiastic supporter of ecumenism wrote an article in the June 1988 edition of the New Covenant on *"Why I Love Mary,"* arguing that *"Her faith is a model for our faith,"* in which Mary is portrayed as the Mother who answers the prayers of the faithful.

John Wimber also has come out strongly in favour of Roman Catholic evangelism, *"Since Pope John XXIII called Vatican II and prayed 'Come Holy Spirit, we need a new Pentecost,' there has been an explosion in the Church,"* he said.[1]

The late John Wimber obviously believed that we owe that which is happening throughout the earth, to the head of the Catholic Church. But he is not the only one! In January 1981 Billy Graham described the Pope as the greatest moral leader of the world and the world's greatest evangelist.

Billy Graham is regularly featured in Time Magazine's *"top ten most respected men."* But **I must say is _respectability above truth?_** He is conspicuously careful not to cause offence or to adopt controversial positions, which might forfeit his close relationship with kings and political leaders, or his near universal popularity.

For example, when asked by the BBC radio program Sunday about Nancy Reagan's consultation of an Astrologer in relation to President Reagan's diary. Dr Graham replied, *"Astrology is all right as long as it is not taken too seriously."* Of course the bible says other wise *(Isaiah 47:13)*. *Yet when Billy Graham began his ministry as an itinerant evangelist, he proclaimed that the three greatest dangers facing the world were Islam, Roman Catholicism and Communism.*

Deceived by the Desire for World Peace

A remarkable revelation from a 1990 book, *"The Keys of This Blood" (written by Professor Malachi Martin, who is described as a former Jesuit),* is that Pope John Paul II believes in his own special destiny as directed by Our Lady of Fatima. He is convinced that he will be called in the 1990s to be the moral and spiritual leader of a world government.

He is also sure that it was Our Lady of Fatima who spared his life from the assassination attempt on 13th May 1981. For it was as he bent over to inspect an *"Our Lady of Fatima"* medal worn by a little girl, on the Anniversary of the first Fatima appearance, that the two shots specifically aimed at his head passed over him.

While he was recovering from the assassination attempt, which had taken place on the official feast day of Our Lady of Fatima, he had a vision of things to come. In the vision, which apparently came from prayer and his total trust in Our Lady of Fatima, and was as an exact repetition of what had taken place at Fatima on 13th October 1917, the Virgin Mother told him that there would be a repeat of the Fatima miracle.

She will intervene in the 1990s with signs and wonders, again involving the son, which will authenticate John Paul's reign over the world... for a short time of peace and prosperity before the return of Christ.[2]

The bible warns again and again of the <u>false peace</u> that the Antichrist will bring:

Because, even because they have seduced my people, saying, Peace; and there was no peace.

(Ezekiel 13:10 KJV)

Jesus said no peace but division:

Suppose ye that I am come to give peace on earth? I tell you, Nay; but rather division.

(Luke 12:51 KJV)

We are instructed to pray for the peace of Jerusalem. The peace that the Lord has promised will come only when He comes.

Who's Leading the New World Order Today?

The book of Malachi Martin, explored what he called *"the three-way race between Gorbachev, Bush and John Paul II to lead the New World Order."* Martin admitted that, since the collapse of the former communist government, John Paul II is working to achieve a theocracy in Poland.

Speaking of the former USSR president, Martin said, "Gorbachev is very comfortable. He has his think-tank in Moscow financed by [Chancellor] Kohl of Germany and assured of funds for the future *(remember Gorbachev may have stolen millions of dollars)*. He has a refuge across the border in Finland and he has no restraints. The Yeltsin regime will not last... *Gorbachev is sitting pretty.* He will surely come back."

Martin, a long time observer of the Vatican, points out that Catholicism in Europe is moving away from traditional beliefs and embracing a great deal of New Age theology.

Speaking about the emerging European Super State Martin said, "It will include all the lands occupied by the ancient Romans, but the religion will not be Christianity or Catholicism, Buddhism, Islam, Hinduism or any other religion known today.

Influencing our Present Policies

It already has its own religion, if we want to call it that. It is called the **New Age**... The environment will be almost deified and sanctified... The New Age movement is at this moment influencing our present policies. If you listen to Prince Edward or Prince Charles of England, it is very obvious that they speak from a New Age background, and it bodes a lot of trouble for traditional Christianity."[3]

The bible describes the worldwide apostate church of the last days as a tremendously oppressive religious power that will form an unholy alliance with the Antichrist to obtain world power. Many of the major churches today are totally committed to a New Age agenda that includes a plan to achieve religious unity as part of the New World Order.

The seventeenth chapter of Revelation foretells the terrifying destiny of this satanic apostate church of the last days.

And the ten horns which you saw on the beast, these will hate the harlot, make her desolate and naked, eat her flesh and burn her with fire. For God has put it into their hearts to fulfil His purpose, to be of one mind, and to give their kingdom to the beast, until the words of God are fulfilled.
(Revelation 17:16-17 NKJV)

Someone said,

"Marry the spirit of the age in this generation and you will be a widow in the next."

❖

Endnotes

Preface

1. Appointment in Jerusalem, by Derek and Lydia Prince, Publisher: Chosen Books, Zondervan Publishing House, USA, 1975, p174

Chapter 1 The Temple and the Antichrist

1. "Word from Jerusalem" Magazine (December 2013 edition), Published by International Christian Embassy Jerusalem, December 2013, p4-5

Chapter 2 Rebuilding in Jerusalem

1. Rushing to Armageddon, Prophecy 2000, by David Allen Lewis, ISBN: 0-89221-179-2, Publisher: New Leaf Press, USA, 1991, p138-139

2. Jerusalem Post, article: "A Place for The Lord" by Pinchas H. Pell, published: February 11th, 1989

3. "Time" Magazine, article: "Time for a New Temple?," 16th October 1989, edition

4. Prince of Darkness, Antichrist and The New World Order, by Grant R. Jeffrey, ISBN: 0-921714-04-1, Publisher: Forntier Research Publications, Canada, 1994, p295-297

Chapter 3 The Prince of Darkness will Defile the Temple

1. Prince of Darkness, Antichrist and The New World Order, by Grant R. Jeffrey, ISBN: 0-921714-04-1, Publisher: Frontier Research Publications, Canada, 1994, p300-301

2. Appointment in Jerusalem, by Derek and Lydia Prince, Publisher: Chosen Books, Zondervan Publishing House, USA, 1975, p181-183

3. Prince of Darkness, Antichrist and The New World Order, p301

Chapter 4 Revival of the Babylonian Religious System

1. Messiah: War in the Middle East & the Road to Armageddon, by Grant R. Jeffrey, ISBN-13: 978-0921714026, Publisher: WaterBrook Press, 1995

2. The Jewish Encyclopedia, Volume 9, Publisher: Funk and Wagnalls Co., New York USA, p309

3. Antiquities of the Jews, by Flavius Josephus, Publisher: John C. Winston Co., Philadelphia USA, 1957 edition, Book 1, 4:2,3

4. The Two Babylons, by Alexander Hislop, Publisher: Loizeaux Brothers, New York USA, 1959; also published by: S.W Partridge & Co. (A & C Black, Publishers, Ltd.)

5. Babylon Mystery Religion, by Ralph Edward Woodrow, Publisher: Ralph Woodrow Evangelistic Association, Inc., USA, 1966, p6

Chapter 5 Mother Goddess

1. New Age Lies To Women, by Wanda Marrs, Publisher: Living Truth, USA, 1990, p106

2. Pope Pius XII, Munificentissimus Deus, No14

3. Second Vatican Council, Dogmatic Constitution on the Church, No62

4. The Roman Catechism: The Catechism of the Council of Trent, by John A. McHugh, O.P. and Charles J. Callan O.P., translators, Publisher: Tan Books, Rockford Illinois, USA, 1982, p46

5. The Roman Catechism: The Catechism of the Council of Trent, p45-46

6. The Roman Catechism: The Catechism of the Council of Trent, p45-46

7. Litany of the Blessed Virgin Mary, approved by Pope Sixtus V, (compare these scriptures: John 15:11; Revelation 22:16; John 10:9; 14:6; Matthew 11:19,28)

8. Litany of the Blessed Virgin Mary, (compare these scriptures: John 15:11; Revelation 22:16; John 10:9; 14:6; Matthew 11:19,28)

9. Catechism of the Catholic Church, http://www.vatican.va/ archive/ENG0015/_INDEX.HTM, 721

10. Catechism of the Catholic Church, 963, 971, 2677

11. Catechism of the Catholic Church, 495, 509

12. The Two Babylons, by Alexander Hislop, Publisher: Loizeaux Brothers, New York USA, 1959; also published by: S.W Partridge & Co. (A & C Black, Publishers, Ltd.), p20

13. Babylon Mystery Religion, by Ralph Edward Woodrow, Publisher: Ralph Woodrow Evangelistic Association, Inc., USA, 1966, p24-26

Chapter 6 Mother Goddess, the Sex Queen

1. New Age Lies To Women, by Wanda Marrs, Publisher: Living Truth, USA, 1990, p107

2. "Time" Magazine, article: "Rock is a Four Lettered Word," 30th September 1985, edition, p70

3. Women in a Video Cage, by Judith Reisman, 1985, p54

4. USA Today, March 30th, 1989, pD1

5. A Goddess in My Shoes, by Rickie Moore, Publisher: Humanics, Atlanta Georgia USA, 1988, p75-90

6. New Age Lies To Women, p57-58

7. The Aquarian Conspiracy, by Marilyn Fergusion, ISBN-13: 978-0874774580, Publisher: Jeremy P. Tarcher; 2nd edition, 1987

8. Promotional Flyer, "1987 International Seth Seminar," Austin Seth Center, Austin, Texas USA

9. Yoga Journal, by Miriam Starhawk, May-June 1986, p59

10. The Spiral Dance: A Rebirth of the Ancient Religion of the Great Goddess, by Miriam Starhawk, Publisher: Harper & Row, Publishers, California USA, 1979, p83

11. New Age Lies To Women, p143-145; see also: The Goddess Goes to Washington, by Donna Steichen, Published in "Fidelity" Magazine, December 1986, p34-44

12. The Coming of the Cosmic Christ, by Matthew Fox, ISBN-13: 978-0060629151, Publisher: HarperOne; 1 edition, 1988

Chapter 7 Antichrist and the New World Order

1. Rushing to Armageddon, Prophecy 2000, by David Allen Lewis, ISBN: 0-89221-179-2, Publisher: New Leaf Press, USA, 1991, p40-42

Chapter 8 Revived Roman Empire

1. Prince of Darkness, Antichrist and The New World Order, by Grant R. Jeffrey, ISBN: 0-921714-04-1, Publisher: Frontier Research Publications, Canada, 1994, p113-115

2. Rushing to Armageddon, Prophecy 2000, by David Allen Lewis, ISBN: 0-89221-179-2, Publisher: New Leaf Press, USA, 1991, p49

Chapter 9 Everyone is Going New Age!

1. Shaping A Global Spirituality, New Genesis, by Robert Mueller, Publisher: Image Books, New York USA, 1984

2. Toward A Human World Order, by Gerald & Patricia Mische, Publisher: Paulist Press, Ramsey NJ, USA, 1977

3. Whee, Wee, We All the Way Home... A Guide to a Sensual, Prophetic Spirituality, by Matthew Fox, Publisher: Bear & Company, Santa Fe New Mexico, USA, 1981, p242; see also Manifesto For A Global Civilization, by Matthew Fox, Publisher: Bear & Company, Santa Fe New Mexico, USA

4. On the Eve of Persecution, by M. Basilea Schlink, Publisher: Creation House, 1974

5. Secret Societies Old and New 1927, by Vivian Herbert

6. Shaping A Global Spirituality, New Genesis, by Robert Mueller, Publisher: Image Books, New York USA, 1984

7. Revelation: The Book of the Co-Creation, by Barbara Marx Hubbard, p114-118

8. When Humanity Comes of Age, by Vera Alder, p31-35

9. Dark Secrets of the New Age, p179

10. When Humanity Comes of Age, p37

11. Dark Secrets of the New Age, p180; see also When Humanity Comes of Age, p37-39

Chapter 10 Rome and the Ecumenical Movement

1. The Battle for World Evangelism, by Arthur Johnston, Publisher: Tyndale House Publisher, Illinois USA, 1978, p259-262

   Latin American Evangelical Theology in the 1970's, The Golden Decade, by J. D.S. Salinas, Publisher: Brill, Boston USA, 2009, p195

2. The Ecumenical Moment, All Roads Lead To Rome, by Michael de Semlyen, Publisher: Dorchester House Pub., 1993

3. The Divine Conquest, by A.W. Tozer, Publisher: Kingsway Pub. Eastbourne

Chapter 11 Experience or Truth?

1. Charismatic Crisis: the Charismatic Renewal: Past, Present and Future, by Michael Harper, Publisher: Anglican Renewal Ministries Australia, 1980

2. Signs of Revival, by Dr Patrick Dixon, ISBN: 0-85476-539-5, Publisher: Kingsway Pub, p58-59

3. The Observer, by Martin Wroe, 4th September 1994

4. A Crash Course on the New Age Movement, by Elliot Miller, Publisher: Monarch Pub, p164

5. Opening to Channel, by Sanaya Roman, Publisher: New World Library, 1993

6. Catholic Herald: 10th August, 1990

7. The European: 14th-16th December 1990

8. Time Magazine: 10th December 1990

Chapter 12 Danger of Wrong Alignment

1. MCSIO Manual, by John Wimber, Publisher: Fuller Seminary, California

2. The Keys of This Blood, by Malachi Martin, Publisher: Simon and Schuster, New York USA, 1990

3. The Keys of This Blood

Bible translations

- Unless otherwise indicated, all scriptural quotations are from the HOLY BIBLE, NEW INTERNATIONAL VERSION ®. NIV ®. Copyright © 1973, 1978, 1984 by the International Bible Society. Used by permission of Zondervan Publishing House. All rights reserved.

- Scripture references marked KJV are taken from the King James Version of the bible.

- Scripture marked NASB are taken from the New American Standard Bible®, Copyright © 1960, 1962, 1963, 1968, 1971, 1972, 1973, 1975, 1977, 1995 by The Lockman Foundation. Used by permission.

- Scripture references marked NKJV are taken from the New King James Version®. Copyright © 1982 by Thomas Nelson, Inc. Used by permission. All rights reserved.

- Strong, James. S.T.D., L.L.D. 1890. Strong's Exhaustive Concordance, Dictionaries (Lexicon) of the Hebrew and Greek Words.

❖

Recommended Reading

- Ad Diem Illum Laetissimum, No14, by Pope Pius X
- Battle for Israel, by Lance Lambert
- Bless Israel for God's Sake, by Sven Nilsson
- Building a People of Power, by Ian Andrews
- Egyptian Religion, by Sir Wallis Budge
- Everyday Life in Babylonia and Assyria, by H.W.F. Saggs
- Fantasy Explosion, by Bob Maddux
- From Rock to Rock, by Eric Barger
- Growing in the Prophetic, by Mike Bickle with Michael Sullivant
- High-Lights of the Bible, by Ray C. Stedman
- Magnae Dei Matris, by Pope Leo XII
- Munificentissimus Deus, No20, by Pope Pius XII
- New Age to New Birth, by Roy and Rae Livesey
- Pagans and Christians, by Robin Lane Fox
- Prophecy Past and Present, by Clifford Hill
- Reflections on the Christ, by David Spangler
- Second Vatican Council, Dogmatic Constitution on the Church, No59

- Spiritual Mysteries Revealed!, by Morris Cerullo
- The Church of the Living God, by Ulf Ekman
- The God of Ecstasy, by Arthur Evans
- The Lion Handbook of the Bible
- The Mystery Religions, by S. Angus
- The New Cults, by Walter Martin
- The Plan and its Implementation, by M.E. Hazelhurst
- The Prophetic Ministry, by Ulf Ekman
- The Veneration of Mary; Our Lady of Perpetual Help; Our Lady of Perpetual Succor, by Pope Pius IX (compare these scriptures: Hebrews 7:25; Hebrews 13:5-6)
- The Women's Encyclopedia of Myths and Secrets, by Barbara Walker
- Toward a World Religion for the New Age, by Lola Davis
- Women's Dionysian Initiation, by Linda Fierz-David
- Wycliffe Bible Encyclopedia

❖

Ministry Profile

Doctor Alan Pateman, an apostle, is the President and Founder of **"Alan Pateman Ministries International"** (APMI), which was established in England back in 1987, a Christian-based *(parachurch)* non-profit and non-denominational outreach. This ministry is now focusing in two main areas: First **"Connecting for Excellence"** Apostolic Networking (CFE) and secondly, the teaching arm, **"LifeStyle International Christian University"** (LICU).

CFE is a multi-facetted missions organisation with the purpose of connecting leaders for divine opportunities and building lasting relationships, to touch the lives of leaders literally the world over. Apostle Dr Alan Pateman has to date ordained more than 500 ministers in over 50 NATIONS. In addition there are ministries, churches and schools who are in Association or Affiliation, looking to him for apostolic counsel and oversight.

Secondly LICU, which was founded in 2007, is a study program to help people discover their purpose and destiny. A global network of university campuses and correspondence students, demonstrating the Supernatural Kingdom of God through Doctrinal, Apostolic and Prophetic Teaching. Dr Alan holds the position of President/CEO, Professor of Theology, Biblical Studies and Apostolic Ministry. LICU is exploding throughout Europe, Asia and Africa, enhancing the Body of Christ

Dr Alan has authored more than 40 books including numerous teaching materials and LICU university courses (30) along with hundreds of Truth for the Journey articles on kingdom lifestyle *(that are regularly distributed globally via the internet).*

He is recognised as an Apostle, Bishop, Leadership Mentor, University Educator, Motivational Speaker, Connector and Author, who has also been featured on national and international TV and radio networks throughout the years.

Currently Apostle Alan, his wife Dr Jennifer reside in Lucca *(Tuscany)* Italy and travel out from their Apostolic Company.

- Alan Pateman Ph.D., D.Min., D.D., M.A., B.Th.

Academic Background

Dr. Alan Pateman attended several colleges throughout his training *(including studying Theology at Roffey Place, Horsham, UK and a Member of Kerygma - with Rev. Colin Urquhart and Dr. Bob Gordon - 1985-1987)* before being awarded a Doctorate of Divinity *(2006)* in recognition of his lifetime achievements by the International College of Excellence, now "DanEl Christian College" *(President: Dr. Robb Thompson USA)* also "Life Christian University" *(Dr. Douglas Wingate USA)* where he also earned a Bachelor of Theology B.Th. *(2006),* a Master of Arts in Theology M.A., a Doctor of Ministry in Theology D.Min., *(2007)* and Doctor of Philosophy in Theology Ph.D. *(2013)* from LICU.

❖

To Contact the Author

Please email:

Alan Pateman Ministries International

Email: apostledr@alanpateman.com
Web: www.AlanPatemanMinistries.com

*Please include your prayer requests
and comments when you write.*

❖

Other Books

Healing and Deliverance, A Present Reality

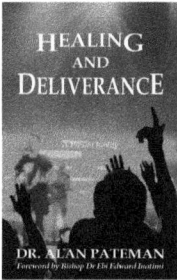

Within the pages of this book (which has to be a "must-read" for any serious enquirer into the Healing and Deliverance Ministry), Dr. Alan unfolds a different pathway, so that the heartbeat of God's message of God's total deliverance can be released into the church of Jesus Christ today.

ISBN: 978-1-909132-80-1, Pages: 188, Format: Paperback, First Print: 1994
Also available in eBook format!

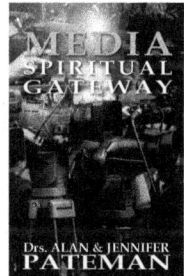

Media, Spiritual Gateway

Let's face it; we live in the era of fake news! It's always existed, but never been quite so prominent. Today it's an all-out-war between fact and political fiction. The media has been sabotaged by political activism. Gone are the days of impartiality and objective unbiased reporting, with many sources saying that true journalism is dead.

ISBN: 978-1-909132-54-2, Pages: 192, Format: Paperback, Published: 2018
Also available in eBook format!

Truth for the Journey Books

Millennial Myopia, From a Biblical Perspective

The standard for every generation is Jesus. However Millennial Myopia describes the trap of focusing everything on one particular generation or demographic cohort, at the exclusion and expense of all others. The Church cannot afford to make this mistake too. Loaded with research, this book takes readers on a journey of discovery, revealing the true nature of kingdom diversity.

ISBN: 978-1-909132-67-2, Pages: 216,
Format: Paperback, Published: 2017
Also available in eBook format!

The Age of Apostolic Apostleship Complete Series

In order to view how the Apostolic baton was successfully passed from one generation to the next. Knowing that through the perseverance and obedience of others - history as we know it was altered forever. Dr. Alan Pateman, a modern day apostle (ascension) looks to reflect on their testimony in this wonderful book.

ISBN: 978-1-909132-65-8, Pages: 420
Format: Paperback, Published: 2017
Also available in eBook format!

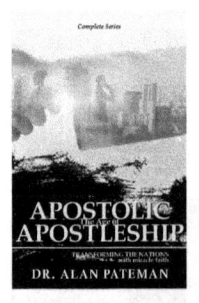

TONGUES, Our Supernatural Prayer Language

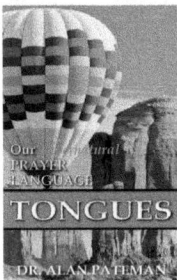

In writing to the church at Corinth, Paul encouraged them to continue the practice of speaking with other tongues in their worship of God and in their prayer lives as a means of spiritual edification. "He that speaketh in an unknown tongue edifies, charges, builds himself up like a battery."

ISBN: 978-1-909132-44-3, Pages: 144,
Format: Paperback, Published: 2016
Also available in eBook format!

Dear Friends,

Have you considered becoming one of our international students? We are privileged to welcome you, from around the world, to "LifeStyle International Christian University" *(the teaching arm of Alan Pateman Ministries International).* **An English speaking university** dedicated to your success; to see you trained and equipped to fully succeed in your God given Destiny.

It is our passion to raise up the leaders of tomorrow, who will have influence in all realms of authority, including the Body of Christ. Men and women of strategy, wisdom and true godliness, who'll stand with stature and maturity in this hour.

It's undeniable that in today's world, recognised education has become indispensable, therefore it is our desire to offer well balanced and well structured courses. Those that have been written by gifted and talented ministers of God, who seek to be inspired by God's Holy Spirit.

Consequently we have put together a **flexible curriculum,** designed both for correspondence students and campuses, which is a strategy to reach the distant learner; whether provincial, national or international. In fact we have many correspondence students from around the world, including a growing number of successful campuses, in various countries.

This is a growing platform, where men and women of dignity and passion, can grow and be established in their God given endeavours. As God is the healer of the nations, we pray and believe that many of our alumni will go on to **become world changers** in their own right.

We are proud of each and every one of our LICU students.
It would be our pleasure if you would join them on this incredible journey!

Doctor Alan Pateman

Alan Pateman Prof. Ph.D., D.Min., D.D., M.A., B.Th.
PRESIDENT AND CEO
www.licuuniversity.com   www.cfeapostolicnetwork.com
Email: info@licuuniversity.com   Mob: +39 366 329 1315

For more information visit our website/facebook or contact our office, using the details below:

Website: www.licuuniversity.com
Facebook: www.facebook.com/LICUMainCampus
Email: info@licuuniversity.com
Telephone: +39 366 329 1315

Partner
with us
TODAY!

We are looking to impact the world with the gospel, together we can do more! Join with us to equip the Body of Christ through our Apostolic Network, LICU university program, campuses, associated schools, missions, conferences, television programs, publication of articles and Truth for the Journey books.

You can become an APMI FOUNDATION PARTNER with a regular contribution of any amount, whether it is once a month or once a year.

- Receive monthly newsletters
- Connect with partners and leaders at our Connecting for Excellence international meetings
- Partners Dinners
- Personal availability for mentoring by Doctor Alan
- Enjoy complimentary books by Doctors Alan and Jennifer
- For those who GIVE EVERY MONTH £10, £15, £20, £30 or more will save money with special discounts on products, hotel rooms, conferences, and more

Partner With Us Today!
Call Italy: +39 366 3291315
Email: partners@alanpatemanministries.com
www.AlanPatemanMinistries.com

All Books Available

at

APMI PUBLICATIONS

Email: publications@alanpateman.com
*Also Available from Amazon.com
and other retail outlets.*

*If you purchased this book through Amazon.com
or other and enjoyed reading it, or perhaps one of
my other books, I would be grateful if you could
take a couple of minutes to write a Customer
Review, many thanks.*

www.ingramcontent.com/pod-product-compliance
Lightning Source LLC
Chambersburg PA
CBHW071535040426
42452CB00008B/1027